DEATH AND DYING

OPPOSING VIEWPOINTS®

Other Books of Related Interest in the Opposing Viewpoints Series:

Abortion
AIDS
Biomedical Ethics
Constructing a Life Philosophy
The Death Penalty
The Elderly
Euthanasia
The Health Crisis
Suicide
War and Human Nature

DEATH AND DYING

OPPOSING VIEWPOINTS®

David L. Bender & Bruno Leone, *Series Editors*

William Dudley, *Book Editor*

179
DEA

OPPOSING VIEWPOINTS SERIES ®

Greenhaven Press, Inc.   PO Box 289009   San Diego, CA 92198-9009

Library of Congress Cataloging-in-Publication Data

Death and dying : opposing viewpoints / William Dudley, book editor.
        p.   cm. — (Opposing viewpoints series)
    Includes bibliographical references and index.
Summary: Presents opposing viewpoints on various
issues related to death and dying, including determination
of death, treatment of the terminally ill, and coping with
grief.
    ISBN 0-89908-192-4 (lib. bdg. : acid-free paper) — ISBN
0-89908-167-3 (pbk. : acid-free paper)
    1. Terminal care—Moral and ethical aspects. 2. Death—
Moral and ethical aspects. [1. Death—Moral and ethical aspects.]
I. Dudley, William, 1964-   . II. Series: Opposing viewpoints
series (Unnumbered)
R726.8.D3783   1992
179'.7—dc20
                                                    92-6667
                                                    CIP
                                                    AC

"Congress shall make no law . . . abridging the freedom of speech, or of the press."

First Amendment to the U.S. Constitution

The basic foundation of our democracy is the first amendment guarantee of freedom of expression. The Opposing Viewpoints Series is dedicated to the concept of this basic freedom and the idea that it is more important to practice it than to enshrine it.

Contents

Why Consider Opposing Viewpoints?

"It is better to debate a question without settling it than to settle a question without debating it."

Joseph Joubert (1754-1824)

The Importance of Examining Opposing Viewpoints

The purpose of the Opposing Viewpoints Series, and this book in particular, is to present balanced, and often difficult to find, opposing points of view on complex and sensitive issues.

Probably the best way to become informed is to analyze the positions of those who are regarded as experts and well studied on issues. It is important to consider every variety of opinion in an attempt to determine the truth. Opinions from the mainstream of society should be examined. But also important are opinions that are considered radical, reactionary, or minority as well as those stigmatized by some other uncomplimentary label. An important lesson of history is the eventual acceptance of many unpopular and even despised opinions. The ideas of Socrates, Jesus, and Galileo are good examples of this.

Readers will approach this book with their own opinions on the issues debated within it. However, to have a good grasp of one's own viewpoint, it is necessary to understand the arguments of those with whom one disagrees. It can be said that those who do not completely understand their adversary's point of view do not fully understand their own.

A persuasive case for considering opposing viewpoints has been presented by John Stuart Mill in his work *On Liberty*. When examining controversial issues it may be helpful to reflect on this suggestion:

The only way in which a human being can make some approach to knowing the whole of a subject, is by hearing what can be said about it by persons of every variety of opinion, and studying all modes in which it can be looked at by every character of mind. No wise man ever acquired his wisdom in any mode but this.

Analyzing Sources of Information

The Opposing Viewpoints Series includes diverse materials taken from magazines, journals, books, and newspapers, as well as statements and position papers from a wide range of individuals, organizations, and governments. This broad spectrum of sources helps to develop patterns of thinking which are open to the consideration of a variety of opinions.

Pitfalls to Avoid

A pitfall to avoid in considering opposing points of view is that of regarding one's own opinion as being common sense and the most rational stance, and the point of view of others as being only opinion and naturally wrong. It may be that another's opinion is correct and one's own is in error.

Another pitfall to avoid is that of closing one's mind to the opinions of those with whom one disagrees. The best way to approach a dialogue is to make one's primary purpose that of understanding the mind and arguments of the other person and not that of enlightening him or her with one's own solutions. More can be learned by listening than speaking.

It is my hope that after reading this book the reader will have a deeper understanding of the issues debated and will appreciate the complexity of even seemingly simple issues on which good and honest people disagree. This awareness is particularly important in a democratic society such as ours where people enter into public debate to determine the common good. Those with whom one disagrees should not necessarily be regarded as enemies, but perhaps simply as people who suggest different paths to a common goal.

Developing Basic Reading and Thinking Skills

In this book, carefully edited opposing viewpoints are purposely placed back to back to create a running debate; each viewpoint is preceded by a short quotation that best expresses the author's main argument. This format instantly plunges the reader into the midst of a controversial issue and greatly aids that reader in mastering the basic skill of recognizing an author's point of view.

A number of basic skills for critical thinking are practiced in the activities that appear throughout the books in the series. Some of the skills are:

Evaluating Sources of Information. The ability to choose from among alternative sources the most reliable and accurate source in relation to a given subject.

Separating Fact from Opinion. The ability to make the basic distinction between factual statements (those that can be demonstrated or verified empirically) and statements of opinion (those that are beliefs or attitudes that cannot be proved).

Identifying Stereotypes. The ability to identify oversimplified, exaggerated descriptions (favorable or unfavorable) about people and insulting statements about racial, religious, or national groups, based upon misinformation or lack of information.

Recognizing Ethnocentrism. The ability to recognize attitudes or opinions that express the view that one's own race, culture, or group is inherently superior, or those attitudes that judge another culture or group in terms of one's own.

It is important to consider opposing viewpoints and equally important to be able to critically analyze those viewpoints. The activities in this book are designed to help the reader master these thinking skills. Statements are taken from the book's viewpoints and the reader is asked to analyze them. This technique aids the reader in developing skills that not only can be applied to the viewpoints in this book, but also to situations where opinionated spokespersons comment on controversial issues. Although the activities are helpful to the solitary reader, they are most useful when the reader can benefit from the interaction of group discussion.

Using this book and others in the series should help readers develop basic reading and thinking skills. These skills should improve the reader's ability to understand what is read. Readers should be better able to separate fact from opinion, substance from rhetoric, and become better consumers of information in our media-centered culture.

This volume of the Opposing Viewpoints Series does not advocate a particular point of view. Quite the contrary! The very nature of the book leaves it to the reader to formulate the opinions he or she finds most suitable. My purpose as publisher is to see that this is made possible by offering a wide range of viewpoints that are fairly presented.

David L. Bender
Publisher

Introduction

"Americans have developed a paradoxical relationship with death—we know more about the causes and conditions surrounding death, but we have not equipped ourselves emotionally to cope with dying and death."

Michael R. Leming and George E. Dickinson,
Understanding Death, Dying, and Bereavement, 1990.

The certainty of death is a fact that every person must at some time accept. How a person goes through the process of dying and accepts death, however, is closely linked to the way the person's society and culture view the process. A person's family and friends, cultural values, and medical and social institutions all comprise part of the context in which individuals die.

Many criticize Americans especially for denying the reality of death. Sociologists Michael R. Leming and George E. Dickinson give several examples of this denial. First, Americans tend to use euphemisms for death, such as "succumbed" or "passed away." Second, many Americans believe death is a taboo topic in normal conversation. People seldom mention death directly.

American funeral customs also point to an avoidance of death, according to Leming and Dickinson. The majority of funerals are handled by professionals. Families do not see the body until it has been embalmed and made to look as alive as possible by the funeral director. Finally, in many funerals the casket is not lowered into the ground until after friends and family have left the ceremony. These customs protect people from having to think of the dead person as dead.

In many respects, advances in health and medicine have also contributed to many Americans' inability to accept death. Organ transplants, artificial hearts, experimental drugs, and other medical advances can, according to physician Robert Buckman, plant "in the back of our minds" the thought that death is "something that can be prevented forever with just another little bit of technical know-how. . . . And as our expectations of a healthy life increase, the thought of dying seems ever more alien and unnatural."

In addition, medical advances have reduced people's contact

with death. A few decades ago it was quite common for death to occur at home, with relatives and friends present. Death was an accepted and natural part of life. Today, most people rely on hospitals or nursing homes to take care of the dying. Writer Patricia Anderson states:

> Death moved out of the home and into the hospital, where doctors practice "death management" and death itself means failure. Science and technology proceed in efforts to transform death from an acknowledged certainty to a possibly curable disorder. In the meantime, people live longer and die out of sight; we can grow up never seeing a real person die, never knowing what death actually looks like.

Because Americans seldom witness death firsthand, then, most people are able to avoid contact with death and dying people.

Americans' denial of death is just one of the issues explored in *Death and Dying: Opposing Viewpoints*. The anthology, which replaces Greenhaven's 1987 volume of the same name, examines the following questions: How Should Death Be Determined? What Is the Best Treatment for the Terminally Ill? How Can Dying Patients Control the Decision to End Treatment? How Should One Cope with Grief? Is There Life After Death? The editors hope that the questions raised in this volume will allow readers to explore important issues surrounding death and dying.

How Should Death Be Determined?

DEATH AND DYING

Chapter Preface

Determining when death occurs used to be a relatively simple matter. A person was considered dead when breathing had ceased and the heart had stopped beating. Advances in medical technology, however, have greatly complicated the question of determining death because artificial respirators and ventilators can now temporarily substitute for the heart and lungs. Beginning in the 1960s, doctors and others began proposing that the death of the brain, rather than the heart or lungs, should define the point of death, and that artificial life support systems be removed when a person's brain is determined to be dead.

Some states responded to these recommendations by passing laws that officially established brain death as legal death. However, many of the laws varied in wording, and some states did not pass laws at all, resulting in the possibility that a person might be legally dead in one state, but not in another. Partly in response to this dilemma, in 1981 the President's Commission for the Study of Ethical Problems in Medicine and Biomedical and Behavioral Research proposed the Uniform Determination of Death Act. The act used the death of the whole brain as its standard for defining death, and read in part as follows:

> An individual who has sustained either (1) irreversible cessation of circulatory and respiratory functions, or (2) irreversible cessation of all functions of the entire brain, including the brain stem, is dead. A determination of death must be made in accordance with accepted medical standards.

The recommendations of the commission became the basis for laws defining death in thirty-eight states, and whole brain death is now recognized as a legal standard of death by law or court decision in all of the United States.

The issue has not been fully settled, however. Some doctors and ethicists still prefer the heart-lung criteria, citing uncertainties in determining brain death. Others have said the present definition of brain death does not go far enough. They argue that the definition of death should be extended to include people such as Nancy Cruzan, in whom only part of the brain has perished. Cruzan was in an accident that destroyed the parts of her brain that control reasoning and consciousness. Her brain stem, however, was still living and able to maintain her body functions. This condition, known as persistent vegetative state (PVS), afflicts thousands of people. There is much debate as to whether such people should be considered dead.

The determination of death has become a complex issue. The viewpoints in this chapter debate several aspects of this controversy.

"A person who is brain dead is dead, medically, legally, and philosophically."

Brain Death Should Determine Death

James P. Orlowski

Many states have passed laws that define death as the total cessation of all brain functions, or brain death. In the following
viewpoint, James P. Orlowski explains and defends the concept
of brain death, and describes the medical criteria used to determine whether brain death has occurred. Orlowski is director of
pediatric intensive care at the Cleveland Clinic Foundation, a
hospital and educational institution in Cleveland, Ohio. He
served as vice-chairman of its medical ethics committee, which
formulated the clinic's official policy regarding brain death.

As you read, consider the following questions:

1. How does the 1981 Uniform Determination of Death Act
define death, according to Orlowski?
2. According to the author, what two ways can the brain perish,
aside from damage or failure of other organs?
3. What three criteria of brain function must be met for brain
death to be determined, according to Orlowski?

James P. Orlowski, "Development of Policies on Brain Death, Care of the Hopelessly Ill, and
Do Not Resuscitate," *Cleveland Clinic Journal of Medicine*, 57:1 (January/February 1990.)
Copyright 1990 by the Cleveland Clinic Foundation. Reprinted with permission.

Of all the acts of physicians, a declaration of death has the most irreversible and profound consequences. Accuracy in diagnosis is of the utmost importance. The criteria that physicians use in determining that death has occurred should 1) eliminate errors in classifying a living individual as dead, 2) allow as few errors as possible in classifying a dead body as alive, 3) allow a determination of death to be made without unreasonable delay, 4) be adaptable to a variety of clinical situations, and 5) be explicit and accessible to verification.

The Uniform Determination of Death Act (UDDA), proposed in 1981, and its predecessor, the Uniform Brain Death Act of 1978, gave legal expression to a concept that had been developing over the previous 25 years. There was a consensus that the traditional heart-lung standard for determining death was no longer adequate because circulation and respiration could be maintained by mechanical ventilators and other medical interventions despite a loss of all brain functions. It was recognized and accepted that an individual was dead whose loss of brain function was complete and irreversible. The UDDA stated: "An individual who has sustained either 1) irreversible cessation of circulatory and respiratory functions, or 2) irreversible cessation of all functions of the entire brain, including the brain stem, is dead. A determination of death must be made in accordance with accepted medical standards."

These guidelines for the Determination of Death stated that "the medical profession, based on carefully conducted research and extensive clinical experience, has found that death can be determined reliably by either cardiopulmonary or neurological criteria."

Two Types of Brain Death

There are two ways in which the brain can selectively die in the absence of serious damage to other organs. One is by severe head trauma with direct and total destruction of the brain. A more common type of brain death begins with a cerebral insult that leads to a vicious cycle of cerebral edema and reduced cerebral perfusion, which mutually exacerbate each other until blood flow ceases. In the process, the brain becomes so swollen that it herniates from one cranial compartment into another or through the opening into the spinal canal, destroying itself in the process. This can happen selectively to the brain even after a systemic anoxic-ischemic insult, such as drowning or cardiac arrest, because the brain is the organ most sensitive to lack of blood flow or oxygen. If the insult is not so severe as to damage all the other organs irreparably, but severe enough to initiate this sequence of events in the brain, selective destruction of the brain can result.

Ordinarily, as soon as the brainstem becomes affected, either directly from the initial insult or from the process of brain herniation, the person stops breathing. The resultant lack of oxygen leads quickly to cardiac arrest. However, if breathing is supported mechanically, the heart can continue beating on its own, despite total brain destruction. This condition is described as "brain death." The remainder of the body's cells can be kept alive for some time if ventilation, fluids, nutrition, and intensive nursing care are provided. The longest recorded time is 201 days. However, during this time, the dead brain tissue softens, liquefies, and eventually entirely disappears, leaving a bag of scar tissue full of watery fluid. Almost always, patients are disconnected from artificial life support long before this stage is reached. "Respirator brain" is the pathological term used to describe the early stages of this liquefactive necrosis.

The Organism as a Whole

The only reason for declaring people dead is that they're dead. Leon Kass drew a distinction between the death of an *organism as a whole* and the death of the *whole organism*. Throughout human history, death has never been defined as the death of the whole organism, because life continues in the body's parts—the hair and the nails, for example, continue to grow. But brain death entails the death of the organism as a whole, a state that modern technology merely obscures by keeping the heart and lungs pumping and the body warm.

William May, *Harper's Magazine*, October 1990.

As soon as brain death became a medical possibility with the widespread use of mechanical ventilators in the 1950s, it became a philosophical problem. Even the term "brain death" is ambiguous because it can be understood to mean either death of the brain in an otherwise live body or death of the person by virtue of death of that organ. State legislators have only confounded the situation by poor wording of brain death statutes that imply that brain death is mere legal fiction. It is important to emphasize that brain death is true personal death (that is, the death of a person) and not merely a legal status. A person who is brain dead is dead, medically, legally, and philosophically.

The Guidelines for the Determination of Brain Death found in the Policy on Brain Death are intended to ensure that a patient who is still alive will not be misdiagnosed as brain dead. As such, the Guidelines are conservative and do not include recent diagnostic tests such as cerebral blood-flow studies, brainstem-evoked responses, and isotopic or Doppler flow studies, which have not stood the test of time and may not be readily available.

However, cerebral blood-flow studies and brainstem-evoked responses can be important adjunct tests to confirm the diagnosis of brain death. The Guidelines also identify a number of clinical situations that can mimic brain death and need to be excluded before pronouncing a patient dead.

The Ethics Committee had originally considered requiring a neurology consultation for the diagnosis of brain death, but such a mandatory consultation was considered contrary to the practice patterns at The Cleveland Clinic. Nonetheless, the importance of the diagnosis mandates that the physician making the determination of brain death be familiar with the criteria and the tests for each of the requirements. Generally, critical care physicians, neurologists, or neurosurgeons are so qualified.

The requirements for diagnosing brain death are relatively simple and straightforward. Only three criteria need to be fulfilled to make a diagnosis of brain death. The criteria enable an accurate determination of brain death to be made in as little as six hours and does not require an electroencephalogram (EEG). The Ethics Committee, however, recommended a confirmatory isoelectric EEG in situations when a patient is being considered as a potential organ donor or when uncertainty exists. The three criteria for a clinical determination of brain death are: coma of established irreversible cause or exclusion of reversible causes of coma, absence of cerebral function, and absence of brainstem function.

Determination of cause of coma. The first of these criteria requires either that the cause of coma be known and clearly irreversible, such as severe head trauma, brain tumor, intracerebral hemorrhage, or a gunshot wound to the brain, or that reversible causes of coma, such as drug intoxication, shock, or hypothermia, have been excluded in a patient who presents with coma of unknown etiology. In these cases, longer periods of observation, measured in days, may be required to establish irreversibility. However, in cases where the cause and irreversible nature of the coma are known, only repeated clinical assessments to confirm absence of cerebral and brainstem function over a period of six hours are needed to confirm a diagnosis of brain death and pronounce the patient dead.

Apnea testing. Apnea testing is one of the crucial steps in the assessment of brain death. Apnea testing evaluates the integrity of the respiratory centers in the brainstem. . . .

Mimicking Brain Death

Conditions that can mimic brain death. It is also important that the clinician be familiar with conditions that can mimic brain death and that these be excluded before diagnosing brain death. Neuromuscular blocking drugs given during surgery, controlled mechanical ventilation, or resuscitation can cause absent motor activity, apparent coma, and apnea, all consistent with a diagnosis of brain death. In some patients, the effects of neuromuscular blocking agents can be prolonged. If doubt exists about persistence of neuromuscular blockade, testing with a nerve-muscle stimulator should be employed. Alternatively, an EEG would assess cerebral activity in the absence of motor activity and would prevent the inappropriate designation of brain death in a paralyzed patient. Sedative-hypnotic drugs in toxic levels and respiratory depressant drugs can also cause absent motor activity and apnea and are some of the important exclusions as a cause of coma.

Guidelines for the Determination of Brain Death

When the requirements of criteria 1, 2, and 3 are fulfilled, the patient may be pronounced brain dead by a licensed physician.

1. Coma of established irreversible cause or exclusion of reversible causes of coma. *a)* The patient must have a known irreversible structural of systemic disease causing coma. *b)* There must be no chance of drug intoxication or significant hypothermia (core temperature less than 33° C) contributing to the cause of coma. *c)* A six-hour period of observation during which tests of cerebral and brain stem function are performed and documented is sufficient when the nature and duration of coma are known. *d)* Longer periods of observation and more testing may be necessary under some circumstances and when the nature and duration of coma are not known.

2. Absence of cerebral function. *a)* There must be no behavioral or reflex response to noxious stimuli indicative of function above the level of the foramen magnum. *b)* Although not a requirement, an isoelectric electroencephalogram (performed according to the criteria of the American EEG Society) for 30 minutes is confirmatory of brain death.

3. Absence of brain stem function. *a)* The pupils must be fixed, unreactive to bright light. *b)* There must be no oculovestibular response to 50 cc ice water caloric tests in both ears. *c)* There must be apnea for 10 minutes during apneic oxygenation or when a $PaCO_2$ is greater than 60 mmHg in the absence of metabolic alkalosis. These tests of absent breathing should be performed following hyperoxygenation on mechanical ventilation.

(Note: Systemic circulation may be intact. Spinal reflexes and some limb movements may be intact.)

Source: *Cleveland Clinic Journal of Medicine*, January/February 1990.

Sedative-hypnotic drugs in toxic levels can produce an isoelectric EEG, adding further confusion in the diagnosis of brain death. An isoelectric EEG can also be produced by moderate to profound hypothermia with a core body temperature of < 33° C and by shock or moderate to severe hypotension. These conditions must be excluded before a diagnosis of brain death is made.

"In the present state of the art of medicine, a patient with destruction of the entire brain is, at the most, mortally wounded, but not yet dead."

Brain Death May Not Determine Death

Joseph C. Evers and Paul A. Byrne

While brain death has become a widely accepted method of determining death in the medical profession, some doctors believe that such acceptance is unwarranted. These doctors argue that traditional heart-lung criteria for death should be used. In the following viewpoint, Joseph C. Evers and Paul A. Byrne argue that medical technology is not advanced enough to enable physicians to pronounce a person dead while the heart and lungs are still functioning. They conclude that great care must be taken not to pronounce a person dead before death of the entire body has occurred. Evers is an associate clinical professor of pediatrics at Georgetown University School of Medicine in Washington, D.C. Byrne is a neonatologist at St. Charles Hospital in Oregon, Ohio, and has written several articles on brain death.

As you read, consider the following questions:

1. Why has the advent of organ transplants made it even more important that physicians determine the precise moment of death, according to the authors?
2. Why do Evers and Byrne object to the criteria used to determine brain death?
3. Why does the case of the pregnant woman described in the viewpoint challenge the concept of brain death, according to the authors?

The question of "brain death," or, more accurately stated, brain-related criteria for death, revolves around whether or not someone determined to have fulfilled a set of criteria is, in fact, dead. One of the questions this article addresses is whether the medical profession, in establishing brain-related criteria for death, has pinpointed the moment of death and whether any doubt exists as to the conclusion of personal death. It is our contention that the present state of the art has in fact failed to pinpoint the moment of death, and that insoluble doubt exists as to whether the patient on a ventilator declared "brain dead" is truly dead or rather is dying and is, therefore, still alive.

It is further our contention, that irreversible cessation of all functions of the entire brain is not necessarily equivalent to destruction of the entire brain. Even if it were possible, using present-day criteria, to determine destruction of the entire brain in each and every instance, we would need to ask, Is this state equivalent to death of the person?

Brain Death and Organ Removal

Because one of the reasons for determining death based on brain-related criteria is to allow organ removal and transplantation, it is imperative from the moral point of view to be able to determine beyond any doubt that the person from whom vital organs are to be removed is truly dead, for someone who is not dead before vital organ removal will surely be dead after their removal.

At a 1987 bioethics conference in Melbourne, it was stated:

> [T]he traditional criteria of clinical death, namely the cessation of respiration and heart-beat, with the consequent destruction of the brain and all organs, recognized that as long as the oxygen transmission and blood-circulation are, by artificial means or spontaneously, intact, life of the organism as a whole, with its essential marks, is present.

With the advent of medical technology and the emergence of organ transplantation, the "traditional criteria" were challenged and new criteria for death were established. It was the report of the Ad Hoc Committee of the Harvard Medical School that brought to the medical community's attention the concept of brain death. It addressed the problem of irreversible coma and in defining this entity offered criteria for its recognition. The Harvard criteria, as they are now known, were published in the *Journal of the American Medical Association [JAMA]* in 1968 under the title, "A Definition of Irreversible Coma," but in the article "coma" was translated into "brain death." Many in the medical and legal community now accept brain death as being identical to death of the person. In a recent survey of physicians and nurses likely to be involved in organ procurement for transplantation, however, only 35 percent understood the medical and legal concepts of brain death.

Most states in the United States presently have brain-death statutes. Because of the lack of uniformity in these statutes, however, in 1980 the National Conference of Commissioners on Uniform State Laws, in collaboration with the American Bar Association and the American Medical Association, formulated the Uniform Determination of Death Act (UDDA). It states:

> An individual who has sustained either (1) irreversible cessation of circulatory and respiratory functions, or (2) irreversible cessation of all functions of the entire brain, including the brain stem, is dead. A determination of death must be made in accordance with accepted medical standards.

Many states have adopted this as a statute.

Confusion exists in the literature over the terms "cessation of brain-function" and "brain destruction." During sleep there is loss of some brain functions, which upon awakening are recovered. Narcotics and toxins result in cessation of many brain functions, which with proper medical management are completely reversible. What we mean by "brain destruction" must be clarified. One of us (P.A.B.) previously suggested that in this context, we use the word *destroy* in its primary sense: "to break down or disintegrate the basic structure of," "to disrupt or obliterate the constitutive and ordered unity of." Nor should "destruction" imply abruptness of physical violence. "For the brain, 'destruction' implies such damage to the neurons that they disintegrate physically both individually and collectively."

Harvesting Organs

The whole brain-dead concept is based on a desire for efficiency, and—I don't think too many people will disagree with me—it was drawn up to fulfill the need to harvest organs.

Andrew Kimbrell, *Harper's Magazine*, October 1990.

The Collaborative Study of Brain Death by the National Institute of Neurological and Communicative Disorders and Stroke, as described by the Committee for Pro-Life Activities of the National Conference of Catholic Bishops in their "Resource Paper on Definition of Death Legislation," hoped to prove that cessation of brain function coincided with brain destruction, also called "respirator" brain. The study included 503 patients in unresponsive coma and apnea. Of the total study, in which 44 patients did not die, 226 brain specimens were examined for cellular pathology. At autopsy "a few of the specimens . . . showed none of the pathological evidence of respirator brain despite electrocerebral silence up to the moment of spontaneous cardiac arrest." "In fact, no more than 40 percent of all the brains analyzed were diagnosed as respirator brains, [and] . . . [n]either the Harvard criteria nor any other widely used brain death criteria were found to correlate consistently with evidence of brain destruction." Gaetano F. Molinari (George Washington University Medical Center), project officer of the study, called this "one of the major and most disturbing findings." A larger clinical study was recommended, but to date, this has not been done.

In determining brain death, both the UDDA and the Guidelines for The Determination of Brain Death in Children call for "irreversible cessation of all functions of the entire brain, including the brain stem." Absence of brain stem function is defined by lack of response to testing of some brain stem reflexes. Temperature control, blood pressure, salt and water balance, and cardiac rate, also functions of the brain stem, do not have to be considered in determining "brain death". There is, further, in the Guidelines for . . . Children a requirement that "[t]he patient must not be significantly hypothermic or hypotensive for age." If the patient is neither hypothermic nor hypotensive and a warming device and cardiopressor drugs are not in use, then the brain stem not only still has functions, but also is functioning.

The Limits of Laboratory Tests

Laboratory tests that are considered confirmatory of brain death have intrinsic limitations. Electroencephalography evaluates electrical activity from only the surface of the brain. Patients who have had an isoelectric recording have been known to recover. Evaluation of absence of cerebral circulation to the whole brain by means of four-vessel angiography is limited in use because of the potential of vasospasm actually causing no circulation to the brain. Also, "the bolus technique does not evaluate for critical deficit of blood flow through the whole brain, only the supratentorial part."

Assuming that all the "brain-death" criteria have been fulfilled, how is it that a patient determined to have "irreversible cessation of all functions of the entire brain, including the brain stem," can be maintained by life-support systems just so long, and then the integrating systems fail and the person dies? While being maintained, many systems are interdependently functioning, including the cardiovascular system, the exocrine and endocrine systems, the excretory system, and the digestive system. In other words, body function and unity still exist. This unity continues for a period of days, even weeks; then inevitably all systems fail and "somatic" death occurs.

Norman Fost wrote in a commentary in the *Journal of Pediatrics* in 1980:

Other experiences and intuitions suggest that death of the brain is not the same as *death* in the traditional sense. . . . Brain death appears to be a critical juncture in the complicated process which constitutes death of the organism, but by itself it is not equal to death.

In 1982 the *JAMA* reported the case of a twenty-four-year-old woman, twenty-three weeks pregnant, who was admitted to the hospital in status epilepticus. She was declared brain dead on the nineteenth hospital day and was maintained on a life-support system for a period of five more days, at which time she could no longer be kept alive. At the bedside a "vigorous" twenty-nine-week gestational age baby was delivered by cesarean section.

When Does Death End?

There is no doubt that total destruction of the brain function means that the death process has begun and is irreversible. This is not in dispute. The question from the ethical point of view remains: when has the death process ended?

In everyday experience, the identity of a person comprises the integrality of consciousness and body, but, as identity relates no less to the body than to the mind, the process of death cannot be said to have ended while respiration and heartbeat continue, the body remains warm and the colours of the body normal. Such a state is, of course, compatible with brain death, and few people would be prepared to refer to a body in this state as a 'corpse'. This fact of experience is not altered by the artificial maintenance of these two signs. They continue to signify that life has not ended.

A further conclusion follows. Where total, irreversible destruction of brain function is diagnosed, all treatment should cease, so that the death process can continue and the relatives, if they so desire, be present at its end.

Bo Andreassen Rix, *Journal of Medical Ethics*, March 1990.

Commenting on this and another case, Mark Siegler and Daniel Wikler wrote:

Now we are told that a brain-dead patient can nurture a child in the womb, which permits live birth several weeks "postmortem." Perhaps this is the straw that breaks the conceptual camel's back. It becomes irresistible to speak of brain-dead patients being "somatically alive" (what sort of "nonsomatic death" is the implied alternative?), of being "terminally ill," and eventually, of "dying." These are different ways of saying that such patients (or, at least, their bodies) are alive. The death of the brain seems not to serve as a boundary; it is a tragic, ultimately fatal loss, but not death itself. Bodily death occurs later, when integrated functioning ceases.

We ask: Is there a corpse on the machine, or is there a still-living, albeit "brain-dead," person on the machine? If it is a corpse, would you not have to refer to it at the very least as a "dying corpse?" Like a square circle, this is a contradiction in terms. You can have one or the other, not both. If the declaration of "brain death" becomes the signal to excise the still-beating heart, the patient becomes certainly and beyond doubt dead.

Inconsistent Criteria

If one is so positive that all "brain death" criteria determine "brain death," why is it, we ask, so necessary to have so many different sets of criteria? More than thirty different sets of "brain death" criteria had already been reported by 1978. Some require an electroencephalogram; some do not. For example, the Minnesota criteria do not require an electroencephalogram, while the Harvard, Japanese, and Collaborative Study criteria do. In Europe, things are different: England, like Minnesota, does not require an electroencephalogram; in Norway an arteriogram is required. Thus, a patient in one locality could be determined to be dead by one set, but not dead in another locality using another set.

In addition, we ask, How scientifically valid are the criteria? The UDDA relies upon the existence of "accepted medical standards" for determining that death has occurred. The report "Defining Death," by the President's Commission for the Study of Ethical Problems in Medicine and Biomedical and Behavioral Research, states: "The medical profession, based upon carefully conducted research and extensive clinical experience, has found that death can be reliably determined by either cardiopulmonary or neurologic criteria." The Harvard criteria were published without patient data. The Minnesota criteria resulted in elimination of electroencephalographic evaluation in a determination of death after doing electroencephalogram recordings on only nine patients, two of whom still had electroencephalographic activity when they were determined to be dead. A. Earl Walker, commenting on this, said that "8% of patients would be classified as cerebrally dead in the presence of biological activity in the EEG—certainly an anomalous and undesirable situation." Elsewhere, Dr. Walker wrote: "Based upon the findings of the Collaborative Study, from *8% to 40%* of persons [our emphasis] meeting different sets of clinical criteria for brain death had biological activity in their electroencephalograms." Furthermore, the Collaborative Study found at autopsy that 10 percent of persons had no evidence of pathology of the brain. Do these reports reflect "carefully conducted research and extensive clinical experience . . . that death can be reliably determined by either cardiopulmonary or neurologic criteria"? We think not.

No matter how seemingly rigid the criteria are, the ease with which they can be bent is manifested in the report by the President's Commission.

> An individual with irreversible cessation of all functions of the entire brain, including the brain stem, is dead. The "functions of the entire brain" that are relevant to the diagnosis are those that are clinically ascertainable.

In one sentence, whatever stringency there was has been reduced to no more than what is "clinically ascertainable."

A Living Human Being

A human being belongs to the species *Homo sapiens* and, as such, is a person throughout his entire life, still when dying. There are attributes of a living human being that do not belong to other species, for example, thinking, judging, loving, willing, and acting. When it is predicted that a particular living human being will not be capable of demonstrating these attributes again, this living human being does not then belong to another species. He is still a living human being, a living person. To say that a patient on a ventilator, declared "brain dead," is certain to die and is, therefore, no longer a person, is to deny reality.

Great care must be taken not to declare a person dead even one moment before death has actually occurred. Death should only be declared after, not before, the fact, as to declare death prematurely is to commit a fundamental injustice. A person who is dying is still alive, even a moment before death, and must be treated as such.

In conclusion, we believe that destruction of the entire brain can occur, but that criteria to determine this state reliably have not been established. Cessation of brain function is not the same as destruction. In the present state of the art of medicine, a patient with destruction of the entire brain is, at the most, mortally wounded, but not yet dead. Death ought not be declared unless and until there is destruction of the entire brain, and of the respiratory and circulatory systems as well.

"It may forcefully be argued that irreversible cessation of upper-brain functioning—or permanent vegetative state—constitutes the death of that person."

People in Vegetative States Should Be Considered Dead

Robyn S. Shapiro

Brain death occurs when the entire human brain has ceased to function. In some cases, however, only the upper portion of the brain has failed, enabling bodily functions to continue but leaving the person unconscious. This condition has been labeled persistent (or permanent) vegetative state (PVS). There are thousands of PVS patients in the United States who remain unconscious and are kept alive by artificial feeding. In the following viewpoint, Robyn S. Shapiro argues that the definition of death should be expanded to include this condition, and that PVS patients should have their medical treatment and feeding stopped. Shapiro is a professor and director of the Center for Study of Bioethics, located at the Medical College of Wisconsin in Milwaukee.

As you read, consider the following questions:

1. How much money does the United States spend on caring for vegetative patients, according to Shapiro?
2. How does the author respond to the argument that some vegetative patients might recover and regain consciousness?

From Robyn S. Shapiro, "The Case of L.W.: An Argument for a Permanent Vegetative State Treatment Statute," originally published in 51 *Ohio State Law Journal* 439 (1990). Reprinted with permission.

Advances in medical science that permit the artificial maintenance of circulation, respiration, and nourishment functions are forcing changes in the way the law looks at death. Historically, cardiopulmonary cessation was the sole criterion for determination of death. Now, however, the vast majority of states supplement the cardiopulmonary test for death with a whole brain death standard, pursuant to which death is declared when there is irreversible cessation of all functions of the entire brain, including the brain stem. The condition of permanent vegetative state, as exists in . . . as many as 25,000 patients in the United States, is today pressing the law for yet another supplement to the legal definition of death. . . .

Due to the development of sophisticated life-support technologies over the last twenty years, society has reexamined and attempted to clarify the legal definition of death. Since the 1968 publication of the "Harvard Criteria" for brain death, a growing consensus has rejected the traditional exclusive reliance on heart-lung death criteria, wherein a person is deemed to be legally dead if he has sustained irreversible cessation of circulatory and respiratory functions. Forty states and the District of Columbia now have statutes that incorporate whole brain death into their definitions of death; and courts in six other states have adopted a whole brain death definition. . . .

Permanent Vegetative State

When total brain death occurs, there is cessation not only of higher cerebral functions (consciousness, awareness, control of important voluntary and involuntary actions), but also of all brain stem functions. Persons who are in a permanent vegetative state are not totally brain dead because their brain stems are relatively intact. They thus demonstrate a number of normal brain stem functions, such as cycles of sleep and wakefulness (with eyes open), the ability to breathe and maintain blood pressure unassisted, pupillary responses to light, the utterance of unintelligible instinctive grunts or screams, sporadic movements of facial muscles and non-paralyzed limbs, and gag and cough reflexes. In addition, cardiorespiratory activity, swallowing, and digestive and other nonneurological vital functions are usually preserved to an extent that standard nutritional and supportive measures will sustain life indefinitely.

Nonetheless, persons in permanent vegetative state demonstrate a total loss of cerebral cortical functioning; they are permanently and irreversibly devoid of any awareness, thought, or feelings. Thus, for permanently vegetative patients, "personality, memory, purposive action, social interaction . . . joy, satisfaction and pleasure [are forever gone]." Moreover, such patients do not and will never experience pain or suffering. According to the

American Academy of Neurology,

> [p]ersistent vegetative state patients do not have the capacity to experience pain or suffering. Pain and suffering are attributes of consciousness requiring cerebral cortical functioning, and patients who are permanently and completely unconscious cannot experience these symptoms.

Permanent vegetative state often results when a patient suffers a cardiac or respiratory arrest causing lack of blood flow (ischemia) or oxygen (hypoxia) to the brain for a period of time. The cerebral cortex is the part of the brain most vulnerable to blood flow deprivation because of its high metabolic rate, which requires a constant supply of blood, oxygen, and glucose. The brain stem, however, is fairly resistant to ischemia or hypoxia.

"The artificial life support systems are intact, but I'd say Mr. Phipps could use a talking to."

A diagnosis of the permanent vegetative state usually can be made with a reasonably high degree of reliability within weeks or months after the original injury by a physician skilled in neurological diagnosis. However, unlike whole brain death, while there are generally accepted criteria for diagnosis of permanent vegetative state, there does not exist one single, detailed, published set of specific and certain medical criteria that can be applied to determine with certainty whether a person is in a permanent vegetative state. Moreover, there have been a few unexpected recoveries of cognitive functions in situations where neurologists diagnosed permanent vegetative state using the generally accepted criteria. Furthermore, there are no specific, widely used laboratory tests to *confirm* the clinical diagnosis of permanent vegetative state. . . .

It is not uncommon for a patient in a permanent vegetative state to survive for five to twenty years. The variable survival periods of such patients depend on age (older patients develop more medical complications secondary to prolonged immobility and unresponsiveness than do younger patients); economic, family, and institutional factors; natural resistance of the patients' bodies to infections; and the effectiveness of the patients' gag and cough reflexes.

The cost of maintaining patients in a permanent vegetative state varies by state and type of institution. For example, in Minnesota, yearly costs are 18,000 to 25,000 dollars; in Massachusetts, costs are approximately 120,000 dollars per year. One neurologist estimated that with costs from a monthly low of 2,000 dollars to a high of 10,000 dollars, and assuming there are 5,000 to 10,000 permanent vegetative state patients in the United States, the annual national health bill for these patients ranges from 120 million dollars to 1.2 billion dollars. . . .

The Case of L.W.

L.W. is a seventy-nine year old man who currently resides in a nursing home. Even prior to his cardiorespiratory arrest in May 1989, he suffered chronic undifferentiated schizophrenia, chronic obstructive pulmonary disease, and iron deficiency anemia, and on account of these conditions, was placed under guardianship. L.W. has no close family members or friends; his guardian is an employee of a corporation which services incompetent patients. In May 1989, L.W. suffered three generalized convulsive episodes at his nursing home, the last of which was associated with pulselessness and an apparent respiratory arrest. On transfer to the hospital, and throughout his hospital stay, L.W. appeared comatose. Within a few days of his hospital admission, L.W.'s respiratory effort diminished and he required ventilatory support. During his hospital stay, tests were done which confirmed acute myocardial infarction, and a tracheostomy was placed for chronic ventilator support. L.W.'s mental status never improved; his attending and consulting physicians have all opined that he is in a permanent vegetative state.

In June 1989, L.W.'s physicians asked his guardian to authorize the withdrawal or withholding of support systems and emergency treatment, including artificial nutrition and hydration. L.W.'s guardian then filed a motion for declaratory relief, asking the court to construe applicable state law pertaining to the authority of the guardian or the court to direct the withdrawal of life-sustaining treatment.

Pursuant to case law development to date, the implementation of L.W.'s right to direct his care must be guided by the best interests approach, not the substituted judgment approach, because L.W.'s values and previously-expressed treatment preferences (if any) are unknown. The best interests principle instructs the surrogate decisionmaker to determine the net benefit for the patient of each treatment option, by assigning different weights to the options to reflect the relative importance of the various interests they further or thwart, and then subtracting the detriments from the benefits for each option. The course of action to be followed is the one with the greatest net benefit to the patient.

Several courts have employed the best interests approach in ordering the withholding or withdrawal of treatment from patients in a permanent vegetative state. . . .

Nonetheless, the awkwardness of applying the best interests approach to reach the decision to withhold treatment from L.W. and others in a permanent vegetative state, together with philosophical considerations regarding personhood, argue strongly in favor of adoption of a neocortical brain death standard. Attempts by courts to apply the best interests approach to order termination of treatment of individuals in a permanent vegetative state have been heroic but unavoidably confused. A patient in a permanent vegetative state cannot experience pain or discomfort from life-sustaining treatments. Thus, it is difficult to argue that it is in the patient's best interests to withhold such treatments on grounds that the pain and discomfort outweigh any benefits they confer. Literally construed, the best interests approach might seem to *require* perpetual life-sustaining treatment for those in a pain-free permanent vegetative state.

A closer examination of the notion of "interests" relevant to the best interests principle, however, reveals that this principle is logically inapplicable to those in a permanent vegetative state. . . .

Pain and Suffering Irrelevant

Since the permanently vegetative patient lacks and always will lack consciousness of any sort, it is not only pain and suffering that becomes irrelevant—whether he lives or dies cannot ever matter to him either. Thus, the best interests principle, which imposes a positive obligation to do what is most conducive to the patient's good, is simply inapplicable to individuals in a permanent vegetative state.

It might be argued that so long as there is some possibility that the prognosis of permanent vegetative state is erroneous, the patient does have an interest in returning to a cognitive state. In other words, if there is a *chance* of recovery, however slim, application of the best interests principle requires that we sustain patients in a permanent vegetative state for as long as possible. However, assuming *arguendo* the relevance of the best interests principle, such an argument does not reflect an accurate application of the best interests approach. An accurate application must take into consideration not only the possibility that the patient may return to a cognitive state, but also the probability that the patient would be severely disabled if he/she regained consciousness. The only well-documented cases of adults regaining consciousness after a year of permanent vegetative state from hypoxia include one person who is paralyzed in three limbs, emotionally unstable, and totally dependent on others for the remainder of his life, and another person who is severely depressed and remains in a "locked-in" condition, completely paralyzed except for the ability to blink his eyes. Being returned to such a disabled state would be regarded as of limited benefit by most patients; many may consider it particularly harmful, in light of the severe financial and emotional burdens that long-term treatment could impose on their families and loved ones.

Neocortical Death

Death is best understood by looking at the actual everyday use of the words "death" and "dead" in our personal lives. Common usage indicates that "death" and "dead" mean someone is definitively gone. It has long been agreed that these terms apply to those whose cardiac and pulmonary functions have irreversibly ceased and, for the past few decades, also to those whose total brain functions have irreversibly ceased, leaving them totally unconscious and unable to sustain respiration and nourishment without medical support. Supporters of neocortical death are suggesting that it is also conceptually appropriate to conceive as gone or dead those people whose neocortical functions have irreversibly ceased, leaving them permanently unconscious and unable to nourish themselves without medical support. While there are important differences between the whole brain dead and the neocortically dead, the significance of these differences is lessened by the important similarity both kinds of patients share: they are both "gone" as far as any awareness is concerned despite appearances of life.

Raymond J. Devettere, *Law, Medicine & Health Care*, Spring/Summer 1990.

Clearly, then, even considering the extremely remote possibility that the diagnosis of permanent vegetative state is wrong and the patient may regain consciousness, the best interests principle, properly applied, does *not* require that permanently unconscious patients be sustained indefinitely. And if the possibility of an erroneous diagnosis is discounted as too remote, the best interests approach is of no help to treatment decisionmakers at all, since the best interests principle is appropriately applied only to cases where treatment or nontreatment can either serve or thwart a patient's interests. Permanently unconscious patients have no more interests of the sort that the best interests principle is designed to protect than do those who are dead. A more direct and intellectually honest approach to terminating treatment of such patients, therefore, may be to define them as "dead."

Redefining death to include those who are permanently vegetative would not only resolve present treatment decision making dilemmas regarding such patients and avoid the awkward utilization of the best interests approach in that regard; it would also accord with philosophical notions of what "being alive" means. Many philosophers have convincingly argued that a given person ceases to exist with the destruction of whatever processes there are that normally underlie the person's psychological continuity and connectedness. Since these processes are those which occur in the upper brain, it may forcefully be argued that irreversible cessation of upper-brain functioning—or permanent vegetative state—constitutes the death of that person.

Diagnosing PVS

Clinical uncertainties prevent the acceptability, presently, of redefining death to include those in a permanent vegetative state. A key factor in expanding the definition of death to include whole brain death, after all, was the certainty of diagnosis. The medical profession thus far has been unable to achieve the same degree of certainty of diagnosis and prognosis in vegetative state as in cardiorespiratory or whole brain death. Although there is no more benefit from continued treatment or continued existence for those in a permanent vegetative state than there is for patients who are dead, nearly total certainty of prognosis must be achieved before a higher-brain death statute may seriously be considered.

Nonetheless, since irreversible unconsciousness can, today, be diagnosed with certainty in a significant number of cases, there should be a strong presumption against medical treatment and preservation of biological functions for a person who is in a permanent vegetative state. As would be true with a neocortical brain death standard, such a presumption would avoid the awkwardness of applying a strictly construed substituted judgment approach and the best interests approach to treatment termination decisions involving permanently vegetative patients. Moreover, it would more appropriately accord with the physician's role and result in a wiser use of limited health care resources. The President's Commission noted that "treatment ordinarily aims to benefit a patient through preserving life, relieving pain and suffering, protecting against disability, and returning maximally effective functioning." A physician's continued treatment of a permanently vegetative patient cannot, by definition, bring about improvement or recovery; and it serves no "caring" purpose, because, by definition, the patient cannot and never will be able to understand or even perceive his care, much less become comforted by it. Thus, since the goals of medicine can no longer be served by continued treatment, the human and fiscal health care resources of treatment are more wisely focused on preserving health and rehabilitating patients who could benefit from treatment.

"Unconscious patients are not dead. A law defining them as dead would be a mockery of truth."

People in Vegetative States Should Not Be Considered Dead

Julie Grimstad

Julie Grimstad is executive director of the Center for the Rights of the Terminally Ill, a patient advocacy and educational organization that opposes euthanasia and works to secure compassionate treatment for the dying. In the following viewpoint, she attacks the notion that people in a permanently vegetative state should be declared dead. She argues that such people are still alive, and that to withhold treatment and food from them would be grossly immoral.

As you read, consider the following questions:

1. What dilemmas would expanding the definition of death create, according to Grimstad?
2. How does the author respond to the argument that the treatment of vegetative patients poses a burden on family members and society?
3. What is the most important reason to reject treating the permanently vegetative as dead, according to Grimstad?

Adapted from "Proposals to Treat the Unconscious as Corpses," a June 1991 paper by Julie Grimstad of the Center for the Rights of the Terminally Ill, Hurst, Texas. Reprinted with permission.

"The condition of permanent vegetative state, as exists in the patient in a recent Wisconsin case and as many as 25,000 other patients in the United States, is today pressing the law for yet another supplement to the legal definition of death," writes Robyn S. Shapiro in an issue of the *Ohio State Law Review.* The article, "The Case of L.W.: An Argument for a Permanent Vegetative State Treatment Statute," favorably reviews a proposal to define "permanently unconscious" human beings as "dead" in order to cease providing them with medical care, and offers an alternative proposal to achieve the same end.

A Ludicrous Proposal

Unconscious patients are not dead. A law defining them as "dead" would be a mockery of truth, a convenient legal fiction. As ludicrous as this sounds, such a law would mandate the termination of all medical care and treatment in order to make a "dead" person die! Even a child knows that it is not possible to kill a dead person, and equally impossible for a person to be both living and dead at the same time. . . .

A fundamental truth is that dead bodies are no longer persons, which is precisely the truth distorted by a proposal to declare certain living human beings "dead." In the event that this insane proposal is enacted into law, a mere diagnosis of permanent vegetative state—even if erroneous—would strip the patient of legal personhood and permit others to kill him or her straightaway, no questions asked.

For example, Christine Busalacchi, a severely brain-damaged young woman, is alive today only because a patient diagnosed to be in a persistent vegetative state (PVS) is a *person* entitled to due process of law. Her father has been waging a well-publicized legal battle with the state of Missouri since December 1990. Pete Busalacchi wants food and fluids withheld from his daughter in order to make her die. He has said, "I know my daughter is damn full gone. 100 percent gone." Pete's problem is obvious: Christine is still very much here, and he wishes she weren't.

Although Christine was diagnosed to be in PVS several years ago, her condition has improved. In January 1991, Dr. Harvey Edward Cantor, a neurologist who had given Christine a thorough examination, submitted an affidavit to the Circuit Court of St. Louis County in which he stated: "Christine is definitely *not* in a persistent vegetative state. . . . She is conscious, she is aware, she is learning to speak and follow verbal requests. . . and one might expect further improvements." Since April 1991, Christine has been a patient at Midtown Rehabilitation Center in St. Louis where she has made significant progress. By June 1991, she was taking most of her food by mouth. In August, her father, who is also her court-appointed guardian, threatened to remove her from the rehabilitation facility unless her oral feedings were stopped. Thus, at this writing, she is once again receiving all her food and fluids by tube.

Useless Eaters

Ronald Cranford and David Randolph Smith advocate that once someone is declared neocortically dead—that is, the higher functions of the brain are gone forever—that person shall no longer have any legal rights or liberties. . . .

Think how much money will be saved in attorneys' fees, court costs, and the payment of expert witnesses once it is possible to remove all rights from someone who is permanently unconscious. There will be no lengthy disputes as to what the patient's wishes were in the past. Just take the feeding tube away. And whether a patient is paid for by the state (Nancy Cruzan, for instance, at $130,000 a year) or by insurance, society as a whole will save formidable sums of money with this new concept of neocortical death.

"Why," ask Cranford and Smith, "should society spend this much money for patients who can never benefit from treatment in any way?"

I remember seeing this question posed in a mathematics textbook. It was a German textbook, used during the Third Reich. The Germans used to call certain kinds of patients "useless eaters." Cranford and Smith, of course, would take away the legal rights only of useless eaters who are permanently unconscious. But once this model proposal has been put into practice, others making the rules for society might well look with keen cost-saving interest at patients who are autistic or otherwise severely disabled, and still conscious.

Nat Hentoff, *National Right to Life News*, April 12, 1990.

What could be Mr. Busalacchi's motive? The Missouri courts refused his request to stop Christine's tube-feeding, so he wants to move her to Minnesota where the standards for withdrawing tube-feeding are less stringent. If, however, she were taking her meals from a spoon, rather than a tube, it is highly unlikely that she would be "allowed" to dehydrate and starve to death, even in Minnesota. Busalacchi wants his daughter dead, not rehabilitated.

Patients such as Christine would have no chance of improvement if there was a law defining them as "dead." Such a law would imply that the PVS patient has no interests to protect, and the patient would be reduced to the same legal status as an unborn child—a "nobody" who could be killed at will.

A parallel has been drawn between the status of unborn children under *Roe v. Wade* and that of blacks under the 1857 U.S. Supreme Court *Dred Scott* ruling that no Negro—free or slave—could claim U.S. citizenship and which prohibited Congress from outlawing slavery. That decision denied the rights of personhood—particularly liberty, and sometimes even life—to an entire class of human beings. . . .

One is reminded of a scene from a Mark Twain novel: When Huck Finn claims his boat was delayed because "we blowed a cylinder," Aunt Sally asks if anybody was hurt. "No'm. Killed a nigger," Huck assured her. She replied, "Well, it's lucky; because sometimes people do get hurt."

Whether or not those who seek a legal means to summarily eliminate supposedly "permanently" unconscious patients realize it or care, *people* will be hurt, indeed they will be starved and dehydrated to death if the "better off dead than disabled" mentality prevails. . . .

There is no confusion about how to treat a corpse. However, a breathing "corpse" is another matter. Dead bodies are buried. Should we bury PVS patients while they are yet alive? The mere suggestion causes one to recoil in horror. Yet, is being buried alive a worse fate than being starved to death? If PVS patients are unaware of what happens to them and cannot experience fear or pain (Shapiro's claim, not mine), what difference does it make how they are disposed of? If expediency and cost-containment are the primary reasons for proposing a redefinition of death, burial would be more efficient and less costly than the slow process of starving and dehydrating PVS patients to death. Would Shapiro be willing to throw on the first shovelful of dirt? Or, more in accord with current bioethically acceptable killing, would this lawyer be willing to provide "comfort care" while the ravaging effects of dehydration slowly kill a patient? Someone will be required to do so.

A Waste of Resources?

The frequent refrain of "right to die" advocates, that it is in the best interests of PVS patients to "allow" them to die, rings hollow as Shapiro argues: "Permanently unconscious patients have no more interests of the sort that the best interests principle is designed to protect than do those who are dead. A more direct and intellectually honest approach to terminating treatment of such patients, therefore, may be to define them as 'dead'."

Admitting that "Clinical uncertainties [the inability to render a diagnosis of PVS with certainty] prevent the acceptability, presently, of redefining death to include those in permanent vegetative state," Shapiro nevertheless suggests there should be "a strong presumption against medical treatment" because, for one thing, this approach will "result in a wiser use of limited health care resources."

To support the notion that providing care and food and water to PVS patients is wasteful spending, an estimate is given (based on questionable figures) that "the annual national health bill for these patients ranges from 120 million dollars to 1.2 billion dollars." Using this estimate, the *daily* cost of caring for all the PVS patients in this nation may be anywhere from a little more than 300,000 dollars to a high of about 3,000,000 dollars. To put this in perspective, consider the fact that this nation spends—*every day*—over 800,000,000 dollars on defense (before Desert Storm), about 22,000,000 dollars on snack foods, and over 400,000,000 dollars on toys. It seems ridiculous to suggest sacrificing thousands of human lives just to save, at most, a measly (comparatively speaking) 3,000,000 dollars a day. . . .

Patient and Family Attitudes

What about patients who are *erroneously* diagnosed to be *permanently* unconscious? Shapiro's answer is: If treatment were continued and these patients recovered consciousness, they would probably be in such a disabled state that "many may consider [recovery] particularly harmful, in light of the severe financial and emotional burdens that long-term treatment could impose on their families and loved ones."

This imaginary scenario is seldom, if ever, played out in real life. Since 1986, the Center for the Rights of the Terminally Ill has kept an up-to-date file containing news articles about patients who have regained consciousness after a diagnosis of PVS. Not one of those articles reports that a recovering patient has expressed a wish that he or she had been "allowed" to die. On the contrary, many have expressed a desire to live regardless of their degree of disability. Some have even amazed their doctors by regaining mental functions and physical abilities the doctors had predicted they would never regain.

Do families agree that they would be better off relieved of the "burdens" imposed on them? The results of a survey of family members of 33 patients in PVS (residents of four Milwaukee nursing homes) were published in the January 1991 issue of the *Journal of the American Geriatric Society.* The two most significant findings of this study, contrary to the usual news stories about the attitudes of family members of PVS patients, are:

1. Family members, in general, wanted life-sustaining measures provided.

2. The majority reported they were able to cope with the situation both emotionally and financially. . . .

Appeals to truth, conscience and morality, though rarely popular, have seen better days. We need to be reminded, when tempted to choose the "easy" way, that God calls us to sacrifice *for* the sick, disabled and helpless—not to sacrifice them to spare ourselves financial and emotional burdens.

Uncertainties in Defining Death

A definition of death that included persistent vegetative state faces objections on several levels. It may be politically difficult, if only because the public may not yet have digested the recent expansion of the definition to include whole-brain-death. . . .

Clinical uncertainties present an equally important objection. A key factor in expanding the definition of death to include whole-brain-death was the certainty of diagnosis. An infallible procedure for diagnosing persistent vegetative state has yet to be produced. . . .

Patients in persistent vegetative state, however, present more of a problem. The main reason is their relative independence from life-sustaining machinery: the signs of life, such as breathing, cannot be explained away as effects of life supports. Perhaps the most problematic aspect, however, is that a withdrawal of life supports cannot be relied upon to produce an immediate cessation of remaining life functions. After death would be pronounced, a living body remains, and its disposal is bound to raise questions.

Daniel Wikler, *Hastings Center Report,* February/March 1988.

The reader might be curious about what the phrase "permanent vegetative state," often called "persistent vegetative state," means. So are many medical professionals. Shapiro concedes that "there does not exist one single, detailed, published set of specific and certain medical criteria . . . to determine with certainty whether a person is in a permanent vegetative state" and further notes that "there have been a few unexpected recoveries of cognitive functions" after neurologists have diagnosed PVS. In fact, a professional study of recovery rates from PVS, published in *Archives of Neurology,* June 1991, followed up 84 patients with firm diagnoses of PVS. 41% regained consciousness by 6 months, 52% by 1 year, and 58% within the 3-year follow-up interval. This study indicates that there may be more than a 50% chance that a diagnosis of PVS is wrong. If a diagnosis of PVS becomes an automatic death sentence, we will never know who might have recovered.

A clear definition of PVS eludes experts, although most agree: it is *not* a coma, it is *not* brain death. Mary Senander, of the International Anti-Euthanasia Task Force, aptly describes PVS as "a stretchy label that euthanasia advocates freely toss about to qualify brain-damaged individuals for death-at-someone's-demand."

Shapiro's preferred method for killing PVS patients—namely, denying them all "life-supporting measures"—is not as "merciful" as the public has been led to believe. Dr. Kenneth L. Casey, Professor of Neurology and Psychiatry at the University of Michigan and Chairman of the first major scientific symposium on central pain syndrome, held in the summer of 1990, told the world's foremost experts on pain attending that meeting, "They [PVS patients] may not be able to do anything else, but they can probably feel pain." He based his findings on evidence gleaned from both the medical care of brain-damaged patients and on legal cases regarding withdrawal of care.

Cruel and Immoral

All things considered, Shapiro's proposal is unreasonable, cruel and immoral. No reasonable person would suggest that a medical diagnosis of a "permanent" disabling (not terminal) condition, especially one that is impossible to confirm, should be an automatic death sentence. Furthermore, Dr. Casey believes PVS patients "should be assumed to have the ability to feel pain." If they do indeed feel pain, then starvation and dehydration unto death would be an extremely painful ordeal. Indeed, it would be cruel and unusual punishment for the "crime" of being disabled.

Finally, the most compelling reason of all for rejecting this proposal is that the Lord of Life has commanded us to care for the least among us, and never to kill. The care of human life is a sacred trust, which, for the love of God and humanity, we must never betray.

"We may wish to give patients and their agents some choice in deciding the meaning of death in their own cases."

Death Should Be Determined by Individual Choice

Robert M. Veatch

In the following viewpoint, Robert M. Veatch proposes that the debate over the definition of death can best be resolved by letting the question be answered by individual conscience. He argues that whether a person can be considered dead when the body still functions but consciousness is permanently lost is a philosophical question that cannot be settled by scientific criteria or legal statutes. This question can only be answered by individuals and their close friends and family members. He writes that enabling individuals to come to their own conclusions about what is death best ensures that all people receive the treatment they wish at the moment of dying. Veatch is a professor of medical ethics at the Kennedy Institute of Ethics in Washington, D.C., and the author of *Death, Dying, and the Biological Revolution*, from which this viewpoint is excerpted.

As you read, consider the following questions:

1. Why are traditional methods of determining death no longer useful, according to Veatch?
2. How does the author respond to common objections to his proposal?

From Robert M. Veatch, *Death, Dying, and the Biological Revolution*. Revised edition. New Haven, CT: Yale University Press, © 1989 by Yale University. Reprinted with permission.

Two decades ago, scholars and clinicians began thinking seriously about whether persons without brain function should be considered alive or dead, but society still seems confused about the definition of death. For most of human history, of course, people have not been concerned with this issue at all. They have had a clear enough idea to be able to transact the business of death: to cover the corpse, bury the dead, mourn, read wills, and transfer authority. But now that technology permits us to treat the body organ by organ, cell by cell, we are forced to develop a more precise understanding of what it means to call a person dead. At the same time, in the contemporary world, these decisions involve a complex interaction between the technical aspects (the business involving stethoscopes, electroencephalograms, and intricately determined medical diagnoses and prognoses) and the more fundamental philosophical considerations that determine whether a person in a particular condition should be called dead. . . .

The question of whether to treat a person who will never regain consciousness as dead—that is, what concept of death is correct—is a philosophical one that can be answered independent of medical training or healing skills. The options are more numerous than they once were. Once, de facto public policy was that the physician should (even must) pronounce death when the patient dies. Everyone knew when that was: when the individual's vital bodily fluids were no longer circulating, as determined by looking at heart and lung function. The new pluralism requires that we now move beyond this traditional policy. . . .

The debate . . . leads me to offer a . . . proposal, which, although it has not yet received much consideration in the public debate, may be the most reasonable and workable solution. In a pluralistic world, different philosophical interpretations may well have to operate simultaneously. We may wish to give patients and their agents some choice in deciding the meaning of death in their own cases. If we are dealing with philosophical choices about what is essential to human living, we may have to tolerate philosophical pluralism. . . .

Statutory Definitions of Death

In 1968 Kansas became the first state to pass a law permitting the procuring of organs for transplantation. The transplanters at the University of Kansas Medical Center faced a dilemma because a year earlier a court case had affirmed the traditional definition of death. With some overstatement of the problem, Dr. Loren Taylor noted that they were able to procure organs at the same time case law was interpreted as precluding organ transplantation.

That same year, however, M.M. Halley and W.F. Harvey proposed a statutory definition of death thereby initiating the debate about the proper formulation. In 1970, as a result of prodding from the transplanters, Kansas passed the first statutory definition of death. Maryland next passed an almost identical bill. Subsequently thirty-nine states and the District of Columbia passed statutes incorporating some brain-oriented definition of death. In addition, several of these states also have pertinent case law, while seven other states authorize brain-based death pronouncement by judicial decision alone. . . .

The confusion generated by the proliferation of models led the President's Commission [for the study of Ethical Problems in Medicine and Biomedical and Behavioral Research] to generate still another wording, the Uniform Determination of Death Act. This version has now been endorsed not only by the commission, but also by the American Bar Association, the American Medical Association, and the National Conference of Commissioners on Uniform State Laws in place of their earlier versions. It reintroduces the explicit recognition that loss of circulatory and respiratory functions can be used as an indicator of death:

> An individual who has sustained either (1) irreversible cessation of circulatory and respiratory functions, or (2) irreversible cessation of all functions of the entire brain, including the brain stem, is dead. A determination of death must be made in accordance with accepted medical standards.

Critics of the proposed statutes for determining death have either emphasized difficulties in technical wording or made misguided appeals for vesting decision-making authority in physicians or medical professional groups. These, however, are not the only problems. In order to accept a statute such as the Uniform Determination of Death Act, it is first necessary to accept the underlying policy judgment that irreversible destruction of the entire brain is indeed death—that an individual should be treated as dead when, and only when, the entire brain will never again be able to function. Some of us continue to have doubts about that basic judgment. . . .

A Statute for a Confused Society

There is still another option. Part of the current confusion reflects sincere and reasonable disagreement within society over which philosophical concept of death is the proper one.

A persistent, significant minority, including many Orthodox Jews, continues to hold that individuals should be treated as alive until all vital functions, including circulatory and respiratory functions, cease. On the other hand, a significant number of people, especially scholars working in philosophy and neurological scientists, are gravitating toward some higher brain formulation. Moreover, even among those who identify with the whole-brain-oriented concept, there are subtle disagreements: over the exact functions that must be eliminated; over whether anatomical destruction of tissues must take place or only loss of function; and over whether cellular functions count. It is now apparent that there are really not only two or three positions, but countless variations that are likely never to be resolved.

Wizard of Id by Brant Parker and Johnny Hart. © 1989 North American Syndicate. All rights reserved. Reprinted by permission of NAS and Johnny Hart.

As with many philosophical and religious disagreements in our society, we have a well-established method for dealing with diversity. It is to allow free and individual choice as long as it does not directly infringe on the freedom of others and does not radically offend the common morality. When dealing with a philosophical conflict so basic that it is literally a matter of life and death, the best solution may be individual freedom to choose among different philosophical concepts within the range of what is tolerable to all the interests involved. . . .

There are two possibilities: (1) we could require every individual (or the next of kin or other legal guardians) to choose from acceptable definitions of death, or (2) we could adopt one definition to be followed unless caregivers are instructed otherwise. The second approach seems more practical.

There are, in fact, several objections to the idea of limited choice among definitions of death. Has individualism run amok? Do we really want to be so antinomian, so anarchical, that any individual no matter how malicious or foolish can specify any meaning of death that the rest of society would then be obliged to honor? What if Aunt Bertha says she knows Uncle Charlie's brain is completely destroyed and his heart is not beating and his lungs are not functioning, but she still thinks there is hope—she does not want death pronounced for a few more days? Worse yet, what if a grown son who has long since abandoned his senile, mentally ill, and institutionalized father decides that his father's life has lost whatever makes it essentially human and chooses to have him called dead even though his heart, lungs, and higher brain centers continue to function? Clearly society cannot permit every individual literally to choose any concept of death. For the same reason, the shortsighted acceptance of death as meaning whatever physicians choose for it to mean is wrong. A physician agreeing with either Aunt Bertha or the coldhearted son should certainly be challenged by society and its judicial system.

There are also practical problems in requiring every individual or guardian to make such a choice. Many people simply will not do so while competent. Many guardians will not understand the complex questions being raised. Some individuals will not have guardians available to make these choices. The more practical solution is to specify some general standard for death that should be used for all legal purposes unless the individual, while competent, or a guardian in the case that the individual has not spoken while competent, selects some other, reasonable definition of death.

A Default Definition

With this approach it will not matter a great deal which of the plausible definitions of death is chosen. It could be one focusing on the locus of the heart, the whole brain, or the higher brain. Any person not accepting this so-called default position would then have the option of choosing some other definition. It would probably make sense to choose the default position held by the largest group in the jurisdiction. And while it should be clear that no single position attracts a majority of the population, it also seems that, at the present time, the greatest support appears to be for the whole-brain-oriented definition. One might also argue that the safest course would be to choose the heart-oriented position, forcing dissenters to register for one of the other positions. I am inclined to favor a default based on the higher brain position, because I think it is the right formulation. Some such discretion is necessary, however, if a society is not going to violate the consciences of a significant majority of its population.

No Scientific Certainty

We may never know with certainty when life ends; we will almost certainly never have 100 percent agreement on that issue in this society despite scientific advances. Individuals must determine where they stand on this important subject and plan accordingly.

Cheryl K. Smith, *Hemlock Quarterly*, January 1992.

The President's Commission, partially at my urging, considered incorporating a conscience clause in the selection of a definition of death and rejected this possibility. Its members argued that "unfortunate and mischievous results are easily imaginable." In the 1981 report, however, they do not cite any such results. They only cite an earlier article by the commission's executive director. That article states specifically that the "mischief that would be worked by a conscience clause of the sort recommended by Dr. Veatch is probably not great." It goes on to illustrate potential problems, but only through cases where a guardian was acting with obvious conflict of interest and where guardians opt for extreme and unacceptable definitions of death of the sort discussed above. Alexander M. Capron cites the example of a man who shoots his wife and tries to avoid a murder charge by opting for a definition of death that would keep his wife "alive" until the murder charge could be avoided. The law deals frequently with the problem of removing guardians who have a conflict of interest. It would have no more difficulty removing a guardian making a malicious choice regarding a definition of death than removing a malicious guardian making any other medical or economic choice, including the decision to refuse medical treatment now permitted under many state laws.

The President's Commission, in fact, discusses some of the adjustments that could be made in public policy to permit individual discretion. It endorses a policy of maintaining a dead individual on a ventilator for several hours after death in deference to family wishes or in order for the family to decide whether to donate the deceased's organs. I am assuming that the commission is not endorsing a trick—a policy of pronouncing death, but letting the family believe falsely that their loved one is still alive legally. If what they are endorsing is a policy of tolerating ventilation of what the family knows to be a corpse, why not change the description so that the individual is called alive during that period? This would show greater respect for the family's position while involving all medical personnel in exactly the same behaviors. . . .

The Need for Discretion

Capron and the commission write as if there is some important reason why "society has a basic interest in defining for all people a uniform basis on which to decide who is alive—and consequently subject to all the protections and benefits of the law—and who is dead." In one sense they are correct. It would be nice if all people were treated as dead if, and only if, they really were in the condition in which they ought to be treated as dead. By the same token it would be nice if people were allowed to die if, and only if, they were in a state in which they ought to be allowed to die. However, there has now emerged a substantial consensus that individual deviations from objective metaphysical moral standards ought to be tolerated in the name of individual conscience. People are now given substantial discretion in deciding whether to refuse life-prolonging medical treatment. Any confusion or mischief that could arise in permitting limited discretion in choosing a definition of death could also arise in permitting decisions to refuse treatment. A person who would opt for a higher-brain-oriented definition of death could, if prohibited from being called dead, still refuse life support, in which case he would be dead almost as soon. States have dealt with the fact that life insurance payments will be hastened by legislating that, even in these cases, payments shall be made at death. If a person opted for being considered alive until heart and lung function ceased, the health insurance problems would be no different from cases where decisions are made to continue medical support. The law could either require that individual's health insurance to cover the modest extra cost or could exclude coverage for persons with dead brains. In short, all the confusion in public policy that could be created by giving an individual discretion in defining death already exists in giving that individual discretion in deciding when to stop

51

treatment. Provided certain steps are taken to protect society from the most serious consequences of individual discretion, it is better to respect individual conscience in moral matters than to ride roughshod over people's consciences.

There must, then, be discretion in choosing among plausible concepts of death as well as limits on individual freedom. At this moment in history the reasonable choices are those focusing on respiration and circulation, on the body's integrating capacities, and on consciousness and related social interaction. Allowing individual choice among these alternatives, but not beyond them, may be the only way around this social policy impasse.

"States need a law establishing a single, universally applicable criterion for declaring human death."

Death Should Be Determined by Law

James M. Humber

James M. Humber is a law professor at Georgia State University in Atlanta. In the following viewpoint, he argues against the idea of giving individuals the legal right to choose the criteria for their own deaths. He asserts that such an idea would be impractical and nonsensical. Humber concludes that there should be a law that defines a single, universal criterion for death.

As you read, consider the following questions:

1. What are the three competing criteria for death, according to Humber?
2. Why does Humber support the use of the heart-lung criteria?
3. What are the author's views on euthanasia?

James M. Humber, "Statutory Criteria for Determining Human Death," *Mercer Law Review*, Spring 1991. Reprinted with permission. (Portions of this article previously appeared in Humber, "On Human Death," *Biomedical Ethics Reviews* 1989: 127-63 (1990) and are reprinted with permission of Humana Press, PO Box 2148, Clifton, NJ 07015.

Until approximately twenty years ago, human beings were not declared dead until they experienced an irreversible cessation of respiratory and circulatory functions. Use of these criteria—which are known as the heart-lung criteria for determining human death—was not problematical until modern medicine invented the means for artificially maintaining heartbeat and respiration. With the development of artificial life-support mechanisms, patients who were irreversibly comatose could be kept "alive" indefinitely. Maintaining these patients imposed financial and emotional hardships upon family members, utilized scarce medical resources in noneffecient ways, and denied use of comatose patients' organs for transplant purposes. In an attempt to remedy these problems, many states have enacted "declaration of death" statutes. Typically, these statutes allow physicians to choose between two different sets of criteria for determining human death. More specifically, determination of death statutes usually assert that human beings are dead whenever they: (1) meet the conditions specified in the heart-lung criteria, or (2) experience brain-death (i.e., sustain an irreversible cessation of all functions of the entire brain, including the brain stem).

Kansas passed the first determination of death statute in 1970 and was immediately criticized as "(giving voice) to the misconception that there are two separate phenomena of death." More recently, at least one critic has argued that the same criticism extends to all current declaration of death statutes, and that we should reject both the heart-lung criteria and brain-death criterion for determining human death and enact a new set of statutory standards. More explicitly, the claim is that we should adopt a neocortical-death criterion. . . .

Three Death Criteria

There are, in the final analysis, only three competing criteria for declaring human death: (1) the neocortical-death criterion, (2) the brain-death criterion, and (3) the heart-lung criteria. If it is true that only living things can die, each of these criteria must take human death to be the death of some sort of living organic structure. When we examine the three proposed criteria for declaring human death, we find that this is precisely what they do. Criterion 1 tells us that human beings die when their upper brains die. Thus, for the purposes of declaring human death, criterion 1 takes "living human being" to mean "functioning human neocortex." Similarly, criterion 2 assumes that "living human being" means "functioning human brain." Criterion 3 is not as clear as either criteria 1 or 2; however, criterion 3 seems to assume that "living human being" denotes all products of human conception in which there is a flow of breath and blood.

All three criteria for declaring human death presuppose different concepts of what a living human organism is. The important question is this: Why should we prefer one concept over the other? . . .

Not a Personal Whim

We have reason to think of death not as a simple organic condition but as a biologically based social status. Since the status is social in nature, there are public and community-wide standards for determining it. This is the truth behind the claim that the decision of when one is dead cannot be left to personal whim. The choice is not, therefore, that of the individual physician or of the patient. It is a choice the community must make, or has made, as displayed in its rules and practices. The physician merely applies this customary or statutory standard.

John Lachs in *Death: Beyond Whole-Brain Criteria*, 1988.

Because a declaration of death statute is impossible to justify by appealing to subjective estimates of value, some may be tempted to argue that we should grant individuals the legal right to choose the criteria for deciding in favor of their own deaths. The chief advantage of this view is that it maximizes freedom of choice, thus reaffirming our society's commitment to liberty rights. On the other hand, there are at least two reasons why we cannot accept this view. First, if individuals were granted the right to choose their own "personal" criteria for declaring human death, different persons would choose different criteria. Alternative criteria for declaring human death rest on different concepts of what constitutes a living human organism. Thus, if we were to grant individuals the right to choose criteria for declaring their own deaths, the law would tacitly recognize that human death was a multiplicity of phenomena. Even more important, such a law would be totally impracticable. Given the freedom to choose one's own criteria for declaring death, not every person would make a choice. In such cases, physicians would be left without any clear means for declaring death. In short, states need a law establishing a single, universally applicable criterion for declaring human death. To fulfill this need, they must deny individuals the right to choose criteria for declaring their own deaths.

We have seen that states need single, universally applicable criteria for determining when human death occurs. We also have seen that: (1) we must give "living human being" some determinate meaning if we are to justify using any criterion for declaring human death, and (2) we cannot determine the meaning of "living human being" by analyzing our use of this term or by appealing to arguments that ultimately depend on subjective estimates of value. Thus, we seem to be left with our initial question, "How are we to determine the meaning of 'living human organism?'" I submit that the answer lies in a consideration of the state's *raison d'être*. Mary Waithe states this reason very succinctly: "According to major philosophic theories of government, the need for protection from harm provides the primary moral justification for the very existence of governments. . . . This view . . . was enunciated in various formulations by Thomas Hobbes, John Locke, John Stuart Mill and many other theorists. . . ."

In this view, the state's principal duty is to protect its citizens from harm. Of course, the state has other duties, such as the duty to provide for the general welfare. The state's primary duty, however, is to protect, and when this duty comes into conflict with a state's obligation to provide some positive good, the former duty must hold sway. Since the state's principal obligation is to protect, it must take care to ensure that living human organisms are not declared dead prematurely. To achieve this goal, it must reject narrow interpretations of "living human being" and opt for the broadest possible interpretation. For example, let us say that state S takes "living human being" to mean "functioning human neocortex" and adopts a neocortical-death criterion. State S would declare humans dead when their neocortexes permanently ceased functioning. Some of these "dead" individuals, however, will exhibit heartbeat, respiration, and brain activity. Furthermore, it is possible that such individuals are, in fact, living human beings. Some people believe that terminating the lives of these beings destroys something of value. Thus, when S adopts a neocortical-death criterion, it both: (1) leaves open the possibility that it is declaring human death prematurely, and (2) destroys something that some of its citizens value. When S operates in this fashion, it does not fulfill its duty to protect from harm.

The Broadest Criteria

If our analysis thus far is correct, states should adopt the broadest possible interpretation of "living human organism" when drafting their declaration of death statutes. This means that states should assume that "living human being" means "all products of human conception in which there is a flow of breath and blood," for this conception is broader than either "functioning human brain" or "functioning human neocortex." In adopting statutes consistent with this view, states should adopt the heart-lung criteria, and declare human beings dead when they sustain an irreversible cessation of circulatory and respiratory functions. . . .

In support of the heart-lung criteria, I have argued as follows:

1. Different criteria for declaring human death presuppose different concepts of "living human being."

2. We have no objective means for clarifying the meaning of "living human being," and allowing subjective estimates of value to determine our definition of the term would be wrong.

. 3. States have a duty to protect human life.

4. To ensure that human lives are protected against premature declarations of death, states should *assume* that the most inclusive definition of "living human being" is correct.

5. The heart-lung criteria for declaring human death rests upon the most inclusive definition of "living human being."

6. Therefore, states should accept the heart-lung criteria for declaring human death.

The Need for a Precise Standard

Convincing policy reasons support the effort to articulate a precise standard for death. . . . Failing to define what constitutes death has numerous drawbacks. Uncertainty and confusion about the line between the living and the dead can result in unnecessary or inappropriate treatment, thereby wasting human, financial and psychic resources. Uncertain conclusions about death also undermine the legitimacy and public support for *post facto* disposition of civil and criminal cases. Will it really suffice to apply a heart-lung standard when the legal issue is inheritance of property, but apply a whole-brain death standard when the question is homicide?

David Randolph Smith in *Death: Beyond Whole-Brain Criteria*, 1988.

In opposition to this argument, critics can argue as follows: States have a duty to protect the lives of all living humans. Thus, if states adopt the heart-lung criteria and assume that "living human being" means "any product of human conception in which there is a flow of breath and blood," they will act to protect the lives of all humans who exhibit heartbeat and respiration. States will hold that brain-dead and permanently unconscious humans are living human beings and they will require that the lives of these beings be maintained. Yet we know that when states act in this way they impose financial, emotional, and psychological burdens on at least some of their citizens. To be justified in inflicting these harms, states must show that their actions are necessary to protect the lives of living human beings. The states cannot carry that burden. Premises 2 and 4 in my argument supporting the heart-lung criteria admit that states cannot demonstrate that all products of human conception in which there is a flow of breath and blood are living human beings. Furthermore, some citizens will believe that brain-dead and permanently unconscious patients are not living humans. Thus, it would be wrong for states to adopt the heart-lung criteria and then use these criteria to protect the lives of all humans who exhibited heartbeat and respiration. Such action would be an unjustified imposition of harm, because states could not show that they were protecting human lives by maintaining the heartbeat and respiration of brain-dead and permanently unconscious patients.

A Dilemma

The above objection has force and places states squarely on the horns of a dilemma. If states accept either the brain-death or neocortical-death criterion, they run the risk of declaring human death prematurely, thereby failing to fulfill their duty to protect human life. On the other hand, if states accept the heart-lung criteria and then use these criteria to protect human life, they do not know that all those whom they are protecting are living human beings, and they unjustifiably impose hardships on many of their citizens. To escape the dilemma, I propose that states adopt the heart-lung criteria for declaring human death and view this action as a mere *offer* of protection. Individuals would be free to accept or reject that offer by electing to undergo euthanasia. For example, simultaneously with the adoption of the heart-lung criteria, states could enact legislation structured roughly along the following lines:

Any person who is subject to the laws of the state of ____ has a right to direct that:

1. Their life be terminated once it has been determined, by any means recognized by the ordinary standards of current medical practice, that their entire brain has ceased to function; or

2. Their life be terminated once it has been determined, by any means recognized by the ordinary standard of current medical practice, that an irreversible cessation of brain functions necessary for consciousness has occurred; or

3. Their life not be terminated when their entire brain has ceased to function or they have been rendered permanently unconscious, and that every effort be made to maintain heartbeat and respiration.

When it has been determined that an individual's entire brain has ceased to function, or that an individual has been rendered permanently unconscious, and such an individual has failed to select among options 1, 2, and 3, selection shall be made by that person's next of kin. Where there are no known next of kin, selection shall be made by properly empowered medical personnel.

Legislation adopting the above policy possesses numerous strengths. First, it adopts the heart-lung criteria for declaring human death. In doing so, it recognizes both (1) that individuals cannot be allowed to select their own "personal" criteria for declaring human death, and (2) that human death should be viewed as a single, unitary phenomenon. The legislation satisfies point (1) because it provides states with criteria that are universally applicable. Furthermore, the heart-lung criteria rest upon a concept of human death that is unambiguous, easily understood, and in accord with past tradition. Hence, if states were to adopt the heart-lung criteria, they would make it clear that death was a single, unitary phenomenon. Even more important, however, the proposed legislation embodies a recognition that states have a duty to protect the lives of living human beings, but that it is impossible to define "living human being" with precision. It steers a middle course between failure to protect on the one hand and imposition of harm on the other. More explicitly, by accepting the heart-lung criteria for declaring human death, the legislation construes the meaning of "living human being" broadly and assumes that all products of human conception in which there is a flow of breath and blood are living humans. It offers protection to all such beings by allowing anyone to direct that their life be maintained so long as they exhibit heartbeat and respiration. By permitting such action, the state fulfills its duty to protect human life by offering protection to all those who desire it. At the same time, the state recognizes that many citizens will reject its definition of "living human being" and that many citizens would perceive a requirement that heartbeat and respiration be maintained for all products of human conception in which there is a flow of breath and blood as an unjustifiable imposition of harm. Recognizing this, the state avoids inflicting such harm by allowing euthanasia in those cases when brains or neocortexes have permanently ceased functioning.

Understanding Words in Context

Readers occasionally come across words they do not recognize. And frequently, because they do not know a word or words, they will not fully understand the passage being read. Obviously, the reader can look up an unfamiliar word in a dictionary. By carefully examining the word in the context in which it is used, however, the word's meaning can often be determined. A careful reader may find clues to the meaning of the word in surrounding words, ideas, and attitudes.

Below are excerpts from the viewpoints in this chapter. In each excerpt, one of the words is printed in italics. Try to determine the meaning of each word by reading the excerpt. Under each excerpt you will find four definitions for the italicized word. Choose the one that is closest to your understanding of the word.

Finally, use a dictionary to see how well you have understood the words in context. It will be helpful to discuss with others the clues that helped you decide on each word's meaning.

1. The Uniform Determination of Death Act (UDDA) states that an individual is dead if he or she has sustained irreversible *CESSATION* of all brain functions.

   CESSATION means:

   a) stopping   c) worsening
   b) hurting   d) continuing

2. One way the brain can die in the absence of serious damage to other organs is by severe head *TRAUMA*.

   TRAUMA means:

   a) ache   c) injury
   b) recovery   d) diagnosis

3. While narcotics and *TOXINS* may destroy many brain functions, sometimes this chemical damage can be reversed.

TOXINS means:

a) vitamins   c) fatalities
b) poisons   d) politicians

4. Laboratory tests to confirm brain death have *INTRINSIC* limitations that cannot be overcome. Some tests only measure parts of the brain, leaving the rest of the brain untested. Other tests might harm or kill the brain, and therefore cannot be fully used.

INTRINSIC means:

a) built-in   c) unimportant
b) confusing   d) complicated

5. Historically, *CARDIOPULMONARY* cessation was the sole criterion for determining death. Due to advances in medical technology that enable doctors to keep the heart and lungs working or to replace their functions, many states have enacted laws in which death is declared when the whole brain has ceased functioning.

CARDIOPULMONARY means:

a) of the heart and lungs   c) of the stomach
b) of the brain   d) of growth

6. A permanent vegetative state often results when a patient cannot breathe and the brain receives insufficient oxygen. While the brain's cerebral cortex is most vulnerable to such an occurrence, the brain stem is fairly resistant to *HYPOXIA*.

HYPOXIA means:

a) excess of water   c) death
b) drug overdose   d) oxygen deficiency

7. In 1968, Kansas became the first state to pass a law permitting the removal of organs for transplantation. However, until it passed a brain-death law a year later, state law *PRECLUDED* the actual transplantation of organs.

PRECLUDED means:

a) prevented   c) publicized
b) helped   d) remembered

8. Brain death is death. A distinction must be made between the death of the *whole organism* and the *organism as a whole*. Death has never been defined as the death of a whole organism, because life continues in the body's parts—hair and nails, for example, continue to grow. But brain death *ENTAILS* the death of the organism as a whole, a state modern technology obscures by keeping the heart and lungs pumping.

ENTAILS means:

a) mimics   c) prevents
b) results in   d) goes beyond

9. The term "brain death" is ambiguous, and state legislators have only CONFOUNDED the problem by poorly worded laws that imply that brain death is mere legal fiction. It is important to emphasize that brain death is true personal death and not merely a legal status.

CONFOUNDED means:

a) clarified   c) confused
b) solved   d) bought

10. Dr. Kenneth L. Casey believes patients who are in persistent vegetative states can probably feel pain. He based his findings on evidence *GLEANED* from doctors' experiences in caring for brain-damaged patients and on legal cases regarding withdrawal of care.

GLEANED means:

a) gathered   c) televised
b) stolen   d) discarded

11. Some people argue that caring for patients in persistent vegetative states costs up to $3 million a day and is a costly, wasteful endeavor that should be stopped. However, Americans spend $22 million a day on snack foods and $400 million a day on toys. It seems ridiculous to suggest sacrificing thousands of human lives just to save, at most, a *MEASLY* (comparatively speaking) $3 million a day.

MEASLY means:

a) lavish   c) possible
b) healthy   d) insignificant

Periodical Bibliography

The following articles have been selected to supplement the diverse views presented in this chapter.

Ronald E. Cranford
"The Persistent Vegetative State: The Medical Reality (Getting the Facts Straight)," *Hastings Center Report*, February/March 1988.

Raymond J. Devettre
"Neocortical Death and Human Death," *Law, Medicine and Health Care*, Spring/Summer 1990. Available from the American Society of Law & Medicine, 765 Commonwealth Ave., Boston, MA 02215.

Sally B. Geis
"The Meaning of Death: Time to Talk," *Christianity and Crisis*, February 3, 1992. Available from 537 W. 121 St., Syracuse, NY 13217.

Karen G. Gervais
"Advancing the Definition of Death: A Philosophical Essay," *Medical Humanities Review*, July 1989. Available from the Institute of Medical Humanities, The University of Texas Medical Branch, Galveston, TX 77550.

Nancy Gibbs
"Love and Let Die," *Time*, March 19, 1990.

Lisa L. Kirkland
"Family Refusal to Accept Brain Death and Termination of Life Support: To Whom Is the Physician Responsible?" *The Journal of Clinical Ethics*, Fall 1991. Available from 107 E. Church St., Frederick, MD 21701.

Elisabeth Rosenthal
"Vital Signs," *Discover*, April 1988.

Cheryl K. Smith
"The Curious Problem of Defining Death," *Hemlock Quarterly*, January 1992. Available from the National Hemlock Society, PO Box 11830, Eugene, OR 97440-3900.

Charles L. Sprung
"Changing Attitudes and Practices in Forgoing Life-Sustaining Treatments," *Journal of the American Medical Association*, April 25, 1990. Available from the American Medical Association, 515 N. State St., Chicago, IL 60610.

Kathleen Stein
"Redefining Death," *Omni*, September 1987.

Daniel Wikler and Alan J. Weisbard
"Appropriate Confusion Over 'Brain Death,'" *Journal of the American Medical Association*, April 21, 1989.

Stuart J. Youngner et al.
"'Brain Death' and Organ Retrieval," *Journal of the American Medical Association*, April 21, 1989.

What Is the Best Treatment for the Terminally Ill?

DEATH᷊DYING

Chapter Preface

The past fifty years have seen a great shift in where and how most Americans die. Prior to 1940, most people spent their final days at home, tended by relatives and the family physician. Advances in medical technology and the increased use of hospitals and nursing homes, however, have decreased the role of the family in the past few decades. Today an estimated four out of five Americans die in hospitals or nursing homes.

These medical institutions have come under increasing scrutiny for their treatment of the dying. While their ability to prolong life has been praised, many critics argue that the result of intensive medical treatment often only prolongs dying. These critics claim that medical institutions, in their battle against terminal illnesses, often provide poor care for the dying. Sociologist Michael C. Kearl writes:

> Technology is overwhelming the art of healing. It prolongs the dying process in sterile, alien environments. It requires the presence of paid, impersonal professionals, instead of family and friends, to conduct the modern death watch. It also produces new trade-offs for death avoidance: the implantations of artificial hearts, for example, could lead to strokes that erase all memories. . . . As one elderly woman observed, "It was a whole lot easier when God made the decision."

The hospice movement is largely a response to this perceived failure of hospitals and nursing homes to care for the dying. The modern hospice movement dates back to 1967 with the founding of St. Christopher's Hospice in England by Cicely Saunders. The first hospice in the United States opened in 1974, and by 1991 the country had more than seventeen hundred. Some hospices care for the dying in special institutions, while others support home care for the dying. All emphasize pain relief and enhancing the patient's comfort rather than curing disease or extending life.

The viewpoints in the following chapter explore some of the debates over hospital, hospice, and home-based care of the dying.

"Hospice is the single most encouraging response to the problems of dying in America today."

Hospices Provide the Best Care for the Terminally Ill

Patricia Anderson

Hospices are institutions and programs that have been established especially for dying patients as an alternative to dying in hospitals. In the following viewpoint, Patricia Anderson argues that, because of their emphasis on comfort, pain relief, home care, and personal counseling, hospices are the best alternative for dying patients. Anderson is a writer and television producer whose works include *Affairs in Order: A Complete Resource Guide to Death and Dying*, from which this viewpoint is excerpted.

As you read, consider the following questions:

1. What is the difference between hospice home care and general home care, according to Anderson?
2. According to the author, what are the primary principles of hospice care?
3. Why are hospices better able than hospitals to relieve pain, according to Anderson?

To date, the most successful contemporary model for enlightened death care is hospice.

Defined by the National Hospice Organization (NHO) as "a medically directed, interdisciplinary program of palliative services for terminally ill people and their families," the hospice vision is, in many ways, the opposite of conventional institutional approaches to care for the dying. The primary goals of a hospice program are comfort and emotional support.

Sometimes there is confusion between the definition of hospice as a place and hospice as a program. Often it is assumed that "a hospice" is a place where people go to die. In some countries, most notably Great Britain, the development of the hospice ideal has been centered in specific institutions, called hospices, designed to care for the terminally ill. But in the United States there are few freestanding hospices. More often, the term *hospice* refers to a program of care rather than a place of care. For the most part, hospice in this country can be defined as a support network for people who are dying at home, with the added provision of inpatient care when needed.

Hospice and Home Care

Another confusion can arise between hospice care and home care. Although the two phrases are sometimes used interchangeably, they really mean two different things. *Home care* means caring for someone at home, while *hospice care* is a specialized *program* of support for the dying that is primarily implemented in the home.

The National Consumers League says:

> Although the differences between conventional treatment in a hospital and hospice are clear, it is more difficult for people sometimes to understand the distinction between *home care* in general and *hospice home care*. Many home care agencies, hospitals and other organizations offer home care programs for the terminally ill. These programs provide nurses, therapists and home health aides to help with patient care in the home. These programs do not usually attempt, however, to provide the comprehensive services of a hospice nor are services generally provided for the whole family.

Two of the primary principles of the hospice concept are as follows: (1) The terminally ill person's own preference and lifestyle are key to all decisions about care, and (2) family members and other caregivers also have legitimate needs and interests deserving of consideration.

The Hospice Ideal

In their book *The Hospice Experiment*, Vincent Mor, David Greer, and Robert Kastenbaum describe the hospice approach as founded on patient needs:

Starting from this broad perspective, then, one would not expect patients and their families to accept the treatment styles and preferences of the medical establishment. On the contrary, it is the "system" that must find ways to respect the distinctive circumstances and needs of every individual facing death. . . . Simple though these principles may appear, they signaled a revolutionary approach in terminal care. Fulfillment of the hospice vision would preclude depersonalizing a person as a "colon," "head-neck," or "lung" to be managed according to local protocol. Each patient would be appreciated instead as a total person who had vital connections to other people and who should not be expected to surrender values and preferences developed over a lifetime in order to die in a manner convenient to the system.

While most terminal patient care in the United States still happens in what might be called the "institutional" manner, the hospice model is increasingly utilized, and the vision of compassionate care offered by the hospice concept has now gained a secure foothold. . . .

The Hospice Program

Hospice emphasizes caring rather than curing. In its pamphlet "The Basics of Hospice," the NHO makes this commitment clear.

The purpose of hospice is to provide support and care for people in the final phase of a terminal disease so that they can live as fully and comfortably as possible. Hospice affirms life and regards dying as a normal process. Hospice neither hastens nor postpones death. Hospice believes that through personalized services and a caring community, patients and families can attain the necessary preparation for a death that is satisfactory to them.

As described by the noted clinical administrator Glen Davidson, editor of the book *The Hospice, Development and Administration*, "Different groups have articulated the hospice philosophy in various ways. Generally, however, all such statements address the following five principles":

- Dying is a normal part of living.
- Control of pain and distressing symptoms is the goal of treatment.
- Both patients and their closest companions—family and friends—need care.
- Care should include support for survivors throughout their bereavement.
- An interdisciplinary team, including volunteers, is best able to provide the necessary care.

The hospice concept implies that death is not a terror against which we must fight desperately and at all costs. Rather, death is seen as an inevitable event requiring and deserving of significant attention and respect.

In order to even begin to consider the possibility of death as an interesting experience, it is necessary to believe that it will not be an experience suffused with pain. Whatever conscious or unexamined fear we may have of death itself, it is compounded by our fear of the pain and suffering that we associate with dying. If we were confident that our suffering could be assuaged, it could change the nature of our apprehension.

Types of Hospices

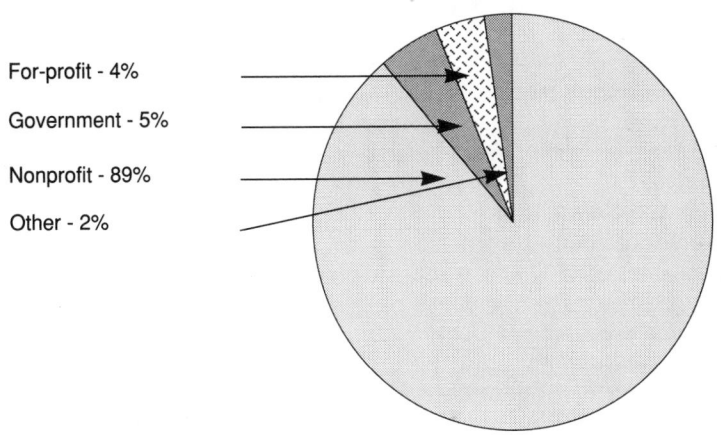

For-profit - 4%

Government - 5%

Nonprofit - 89%

Other - 2%

Source: National Hospice Organization Survey, 1991.

Describing the development of hospice, Mor, Greer, and Kastenbaum state: "The hospice vision centered on a person who was not distracted by suffering and the fear of suffering and therefore could still think clearly and maintain significant interpersonal relationships."

Very often our assumption is that terminal illness (especially cancer) is pain filled, and sometimes it is, but even when that is the case, pain can almost always be controlled if treated properly and attentively. In her book *The Hospice Alternative: A New Context for Death and Dying*, Anne Munely points out that there is

> a widespread cultural fear that a death due to cancer is a death riddled with agonizing physical pain. In reality, pain studies of terminal patients refute this notion. As many as 50 percent of those dying from all malignancies have no physical pain at all; another 10 percent have mild pain; and the re-

maining 40 percent experience severe or intractable pain. Many effective techniques have been developed to alleviate mild and even intractable pain; but analgesics must be artfully tailored to the needs of the individual patient. . . .

You might expect the most effective pain control to be available in hospitals or specialized medical institutions. The truth of the matter is that the acute-care hospital is not very practiced in the more discriminating aspects of modern pain management and can be inadequate in providing *terminal* pain and symptom control.

Hospitals Ineffective

Why? There are a number of reasons, not the least of which is that pain is a rather complicated phenomenon. Controlling pain demands very particular attention to subtle factors. Speaking generally, pain can be divided into two categories: (1) the acute pain of trauma or the "resolving" pain after surgery, which may be intense but has a limited duration, and (2) the long-term, chronic, or "terminal" pain that is the result of the deterioration of organs or bodily functions or other conditions that will not improve.

The management of terminal pain is a special science. But unfortunately, many physicians do not know the latest techniques of this specialty. Doctors and nurses accustomed to dealing with standard remedies for acute pain may not know enough about different types of medication and how to assess and prescribe them as pain changes during the progression of disease. According to Harry van Bommel, the author of *Choices: For People Who Have a Terminal Illness, Their Families and Their Caregivers*, "Pain and symptom control is a relatively new field requiring specialized training. A family physician, or a specialist in cancer or heart diseases, while knowledgeable, may not know the latest techniques of pain and symptom control."

Studies have shown that common assumptions about addiction and tolerance of opiate or other pain-relieving drugs do not apply in terminal or chronic pain cases, especially if drugs are administered in the proper dosage at the proper time. And yet these assumptions are still widely held among many health care professionals.

In addition, the effective management of terminal pain requires, as Dr. Cicely Saunders puts it, imagination and persistence. The priorities of many institutions demand systematic routines and procedures that tend to work against assessment of an individual's particular pattern of pain. Drugs are given at standardized intervals that do not necessarily correspond to need. Harry van Bommel puts it succinctly: "The secret to pain control is giving the right drug, in the right amount, in the right way and at the right time." This demands a degree of individuation that is hard to maintain in the average medical facility.

Sandol Stoddard (author of *The Hospice Movement, A Better Way of Caring for the Dying*) writes about pain management in large medical institutions:

> Morphine shots and heavy doses of tranquilizers, administered in a clockwork pattern in an automatic and impersonal atmosphere, tend to make screaming addicts or deeply depressed or helpless "vegetable" cases out of dying people who, with the right kind of care and medication, might otherwise be quite serene, clear-headed and comfortable.

In some hospice programs patients keep their own "pain charts," also known as "comfort charts," and dispense their own medicine. This allows for a great sense of personal control over pain. Such an approach is amazingly effective in providing relief not only from pain but from the fear that comes from lack of control as well. Experience has shown conclusively that when you allay the fear of pain, you reduce the amount of drugs necessary to control it.

Comforting the Patient

The hospice approach to pain management can significantly change the experience of terminal illness. In fact, the development over the last twenty years of the specialized field of pain management and symptom control is a direct result of the work of hospice professionals in this area.

In addition to pain management, hospice gives priority to the control and management of "distressing" symptoms, such as nausea, vomiting, diarrhea, bleeding, coughing, etc. Much of the physical suffering that comes with terminal illness stems from discomfort secondary to the primary disease, such as muscle spasms, headaches, difficulty with digestion or elimination, or side effects from medications. Because nutritional and digestive problems are often intrinsic to illness, some hospices offer dietary counseling to family members, instructing them on how to keep the patient appropriately nourished. Hospice care includes special attention to the relief of such problems.

Comfort is a primary goal. Hospice care doesn't try to keep you from dying, but it does try to keep you from doing so in terrible pain or in a humiliating condition. The idea is to make dying less horrific in its particulars so that each individual can approach the inevitable as they find it in themselves to do so.

Another principle of hospice care involves the family, along with the patient, as a single unit of concern to the professional staff. It is assumed that the well-being of the patient is most likely achieved in cooperation with the family, friends, or loved ones who are looking after the patient. At the very least, hospice can ensure that those who care will not be shut out of the process or relegated to a role of background handwringing or helplessness. The standards and principles of hospice as defined by the NHO state: "The family members are seen both as primary caregivers and as needing care and support so that their own stresses and concerns may be addressed."

A hospice interdisciplinary team offers encouragement, advice, support, assistance, and an opportunity to rest. Support is provided by groups of professionals and volunteers comprising what is called an "interdisciplinary team." These teams include doctors, nurses, social workers, psychiatrists or psychological counselors, physical therapists, music and art therapists, home health aides, clergy members, and volunteers.

Hospices and Children

Children's hospice care provides much-needed services by encouraging the ongoing involvement of family members and health care professionals with the dying child, and implementing practical knowledge of effective and appropriate palliative measures in children with life-threatening conditions. The hospice concept of care involves an interdisciplinary team working together to provide appropriate medical, psychosocial, and spiritual support. Application of the hospice concept can significantly enhance the lives of dying children, their families, and health care providers.

Ann Armstrong-Dailey, in *Children and Death*, 1991.

Generally, the hospice team works with the "primary caregiver" (the individual predominantly responsible for caring for the patient), in the home, to coordinate assistance as it is needed and requested. In cases in which there is no primary caregiver, the hospice program may be able to help find some support, but this depends on the size, resources, and policy of the particular program. Some hospice groups cannot take on a patient unless there is a primary caregiver available.

The hospice team *physician* shifts the focus of medical care from treatments aimed at cure to treatments aimed at relieving pain and other distressing symptoms. The hospice *nurse* makes regular visits to monitor the patient's physical condition, provides instruction and expertise in symptom management, supervises home health aides, and provides emotional support. *Physical, speech, art, and music therapists* assist patients as is appropriate. These other team members visit the patient on an as-needed basis.

In addition to these regularly scheduled visits, most hospice programs have a nurse on call twenty-four hours a day, seven days a week. As described in *A Consumer Guide to Hospice Care*,

> It is important to remember that 24-hour *availability* does not mean 24-hour *presence*. Hospice physicians and nurses direct and coordinate health care, assisting and supporting whoever is taking care of the patient. But hospices rarely routinely have the resources to offer around-the-clock direct care. On the other hand, not many hospice patients require around-the-clock skilled medical care. The hospice doctors and nurses are available by telephone and, when necessary, someone will come out to the house.

This permits family members to phone for advice or assistance whenever an emergency arises or the patient's symptoms intensify. A nurse may go to the patient's home, if necessary, or may arrange admission to an inpatient unit. . . .

The Hope of Hospice

When we are dying we need support, warmth and compassion, surcease from pain, and help with distressing symptoms. Our families and loved ones need understanding, assistance, and a break. The purpose of hospice is to fill those needs. Hospice professionals are dedicated to practicing medicine in a way that gives comfort and a good quality of life for patients who are dying (while including the family in the circle of caregiving). Hospice is the single most encouraging response to the problems of dying in America today. For many it has already answered a tremendous need.

====
"Hospices can sometimes be a mixed blessing."
====

Hospices May Not Provide the Best Care for the Terminally Ill

Vicki Brower

Vicki Brower is a free-lance writer based in New York City. In the following viewpoint, she describes the disturbing experiences of her mother in a hospice program. She argues that hospices may not always provide the best care for dying patients because of a lack of money, poor medical supervision, inadequate personnel training and a rigid philosophy that compels people to "accept" death rather than embrace life.

As you read, consider the following questions:

1. What complaints did Brower have about her mother's hospice treatment?
2. According to the author, how has Medicare affected the hospice movement?
3. What objections does Brower have to the ideas of Elisabeth Kübler-Ross?

Vicki Brower, "The Right Way to Die," *Health*, June 1991. Reprinted with the author's permission.

Each year, thousands of Americans choose hospice care for themselves or for those they love, believing it to be the most compassionate way of tending to the terminally ill. Small wonder, since experts say the chief goal of a hospice is to make the transition from life to death as peaceful as possible for both the patient and family.

But as I discovered in 1989 during my mother's battle with terminal lung cancer, hospices can sometimes be a mixed blessing. In the difficult last days of a patient's life, the good intentions of these institutions may go awry for many reasons, including financial considerations, severe Medicare restrictions, poor medical supervision and poorly trained personnel who interpret hospice philosophy too rigidly.

Part of the problem is that policies and guidelines to guarantee quality have evolved only recently, so services are inconsistent. Some hospices are far better than others. "We have learned a lot since hospices began, and we are always learning," says Sarah Gorodezky, director of the Alive Hospice of Nashville in Tennessee. "But there is still plenty to do as far as quality assurance goes."

Confronting Mortality

During my mother's second hospitalization for lung cancer in April 1989, we learned that nothing more could be done to stop the disease. Mom was going to have to be discharged to free up a bed. I was her closest child, so I took on the responsibility of investigating her options. Because Mom wanted to be home, and because of recommendations by doctors and friends, we opted for at-home hospice care. I learned that *most* hospice patients actually remain in their own residences. They have 24-hour access to help by phone and, when necessary, can be brought to an in-hospice unit for emergency medical or respite care (short-term residence).

From the literature I read, I understood that "hospice" represents a concept of care rather than a place. According to hospice philosophy, curative attempts and "heroic" life-saving measures, such as placing a patient on a respirator, are shunned once death is seen as inevitable. Instead, all efforts are devoted to helping the patient live as fully and comfortably as possible up to the moment of death. For example, the hospice health-care team has special training in pain management and a relatively free hand in dispensing palliative drugs. Many hospitals and nursing homes, in fact, have adapted hospice's advanced pain control techniques. "The point is to improve the patient's quality of life, not to extend life," says Ira J. Bates, Ph.D., consultant to the National Hospice Organization in Arlington, Virginia.

Hospice care started as an alternative movement in the mid-

'70s but has evolved into a part of the mainstream health industry. In 1983, Congress voted to accept hospice care as a Medicare benefit, and according to the 1990 National Hospice Census, today some 1,500 hospice programs in the United States serve about 200,000 patients. Such programs are now administered not only by free-standing hospice facilities, but also by certain hospitals and other health-care agencies. Unlike traditional approaches such as nursing home care, hospices assign each patient a coordinated, interdisciplinary team—not just a doctor and nurse, but also a social worker and a volunteer (part counselor, part gofer), as well as a religious advisor if the patient wants one. In most cases, these team members make regular house calls to at-home patients. Generally, everyone on the team is trained to work with the dying. "The hospital model gets turned upside down," explains Bates. "A hospital is designed to work around the needs of employees; patients have to eat, sleep and wake up according to a schedule. But in a hospice, care is specifically designed to meet the physical and emotional needs of the patient and family."

Inconclusive Evidence

Although hospice philosophy is appealing, evidence to support its purported advantages over conventional care is mixed. The National Hospice Study followed up 1754 terminal cancer patients in 40 hospices (20 hospital based and 20 home care) and 14 conventional care settings from 1981 through 1983 and found that the quality of life was similar for patients in hospice and conventional care. Pain and symptom control were somewhat better in the inpatient hospices than in conventional care or home care hospices. Hospice patients were more likely to die at home and their families to be satisfied with that outcome, but family members were under more stress in home care hospices.

Jill Rhymes, *JAMA*, July 18, 1990.

Based on my research, I felt confident that hospice care was the best choice for my mother. I contacted a highly recommended New York-area program by phone, and spoke with the nurse who served as intake coordinator. After I described Mom's terminal condition, she said, "Your mother sounds like a perfect candidate for the program." But during our face-to-face interview a few days later the nurse changed her tune. She asked me about my mother's attitude toward her illness and impending death. "Mom's fighting. She still loves life, and she's not ready to die," I told her. The nurse slowly shook her head and said, "That's too bad. Her attitude isn't realistic or appropriate."

Although small and frail in appearance, Mom had long ago earned the family nickname "Moose" for her feistiness and tenacity. Thirty-five years earlier, she had developed paralysis in her legs because of a tumor. After a maze of tests, surgery and radiation, she began to recover, only to learn she was pregnant. Fearing the baby would be damaged by all she'd been through, the physicians advised her to have an abortion. She refused, relying on her gut feeling that she and the baby would be fine. If she had listened to the doctors, I never would have been born. So now, if she wanted to battle for her life in the same way she'd battled for mine, I was certainly going to stand by her. "What right have you to decide what's 'appropriate' for my mother or anyone else?" I snapped at the nurse. She seemed taken aback but didn't say a word.

I worried that if this woman's rigidity toward patients was typical of hospice workers, it might affect medical choices, hastening Mom's death or adding to her misery. "If my mother had trouble breathing because of fluid around the lung, would the doctor tap [drain] it?" I asked in trepidation. Mom had had three surgical taps in the past, and they had given her almost instant relief. The procedure was commonly used to give lung cancer patients comfort, and not considered curative or heroic.

The nurse looked at me quizzically and asked, "Why would you want to put your mother through that?" Incredulous, I explained the obvious—that the tap would make Mom more comfortable and might even allow her to live a little longer. "Why would you want her to live longer in her condition?" she pressed. "It sounds as though she may not be right for our program after all."

Low Points

In retrospect, the nurse may have been right—maybe we weren't ideal hospice candidates. But for many reasons, the hospice still seemed the best option open to us, so we entered the program. In the three months leading up my mother's death, I questioned my decision many times. My mother and I repeatedly faced criticism, indifference and even negligence, stemming from the same attitude the intake nurse had shown—the idea that Mom should just embrace death quietly and peacefully. It wasn't until later that I found out that other hospice patients and their families are sometimes treated this way, because of problems rooted in the hospice system itself. Here are some of our low points:

• Medicare rules stated that before Mom could be accepted for hospice coverage, she had to give her signed "informed consent" to forgo any curative treatment. The hospice program also had her sign a "do not resuscitate" order and other stipulations that no mechanical life supports would be used. If that wasn't rubbing her nose in death enough, she was also shown a pamphlet which noted that patients who enter hospices must have a very limited life expectancy. Under federal law, Medicare-funded hospices must get a physician's signed statement that a prospective patient is not expected to live longer than six months. (This is part of Medicare's attempt to keep costs down.) Though not a legal requirement, many hospices advise the patient of this time frame as part of the preparation for death. My mother and I expressed displeasure at all the emphasis on death, and my mother announced bluntly, "No one's going to tell me when to die." A hospice worker later admitted that we were labeled "difficult" from then on.

"Most hospice patients understand and accept that their condition is terminal," says Jill Rhymes, M.D., hospice medical director at the VNA Hospice of Chicago. "If not, they don't belong in a hospice."

Poor Service

• Being branded as we were seemed to slow the response to our phone calls and requests. It took weeks of urging on our part before the head social worker, who saw us only once every two weeks, assigned us a counselor who could come more often to help Mom with her panic and depression. A staffer finally informed us that we'd been stalled for so long out of fear that we were "too hard for anyone but the head social worker to handle." According to Gorodezky, patients who question hospice policy or fail to adhere to certain core hospice beliefs risk being labelled in this way. A woman called Joan told me the same thing happened to her and her friend Laurie [these names have been changed], who received care from another hospice in the months leading up to her death from metastatic cancer. The nurses labeled Laurie "difficult" because she didn't want to see a social worker at all, and because she occasionally balked at taking her pain medication.

• Medical care for my mother was abysmal. In the three months before her death, the hospice doctor visited just once despite a number of urgent requests. The hospice home-care attendants who did come twice a week were often poorly trained; and since they changed from week to week, I constantly had to brief them on Mom's medication and oxygen. Also, on two occasions when Mom had extreme difficulty breathing, I frantically called the hospice, but neither an ambulance nor a nurse was sent, nor was I given medical instructions. One nurse told me outright, "There's nothing we can do." And once, when I called in the middle of the night, the nurse merely told me to wait until morning, then hung up on me when I asked to speak to her supervisor.

Again, Joan and Laurie had a similar experience. Three times in the first week and a half of care, the home-care aides didn't show up or even call. "I was at work once when I found out Laurie was home alone, and I had to rush back," Joan told me. "The hospice should have made a greater effort to provide reliable help."

"Many hospice programs are nurse- and volunteer-dominated, with marginal physician involvement," explains Balfour M. Mount, M.D., director of palliative care at McGill University Faculty of Medicine in Montreal, Canada. "Consequently, they're medically impoverished. It's a form of neglect throughout the hospice system."

Questionable Quality

Obviously, this wasn't how hospice care was meant to be. Nearly 25 years ago, Cicely Saunders founded the hospice movement in Great Britain on the ideal of "humane and compassionate care" for the terminally ill. In 1969, psychiatrist Elisabeth Kübler-Ross, M.D., published the seminal book *On Death and Dying* (Macmillan), which became the unofficial manifesto of the hospice movement. Kübler-Ross suggested that dying is a "journey," a complex process which encompasses specific emotional steps: disbelief, denial, bargaining, anger, grief, and finally acceptance. This process "requires assistance," Gorodezky points out. "Not all patients arrive at acceptance— there's not a 'right' or 'wrong' way to die in true hospice philosophy," she says. "But by helping to alleviate pain and discomfort and offering psycho-social support, the hospice reduces the patient's and family's fear of abandonment and makes them closer and more secure. . . ."

Some studies, however, have raised questions about how well hospices perform their mission. For example, the National Hospice Study, conducted by Brown University from 1981 to 1983, followed 1,754 terminal cancer patients in 20 in-hospice settings, 20 home-care hospices and 14 conventional-care situations. Based on the patients' own judgments, the study showed that while the "quality of death"—the last three days of life—was significantly better for hospice patients, the "quality of life" throughout the period of care was not.

This and other studies have also shown that, contrary to what I had been told by some experts, in-hospice may be in some ways better than home-hospice care: Because of the more comprehensive, more immediate support patients can receive in-hospice, pain and symptom control may be better, and both family members and caregivers are under less stress.

Hospice advocates such as Bates insist that because the National Hospice Study was completed several years ago, and because hospices have improved since then, the study's results mean little today; but the findings certainly reflect my mother's experience just two years ago. Patrice O'Connor, former director of St. Luke's-Roosevelt Hospital's Palliative Care Center in New York City, believes that quality of life for hospice patients can sometimes be far lower than it should be. And patients such as my Mom and Laurie may find that a gap indeed still exists between in-hospice care and at-home hospice care.

Hospice Is Not for Everyone

There are many terminally ill people for whom the hospice is not the answer. Some insist that their doctors are wrong and that they will beat the odds. Some, refusing to give up the fight, turn to every unproven drug or medical procedure that they hear of, hoping it will turn out to be the magic nostrum. Some enroll themselves in experimental programs for an entirely selfless reason: wanting medical science to learn from their death so that their dying will make a positive contribution to humanity.

Sylvia A. Lack, in *American Legion Magazine*, July 1988.

If my mother had been in-hospice, for example, or at least had more access to a hospice doctor, getting a lung tap to increase her comfort might have aroused less resistance. In general, help might have been more readily available during her breathing crises and depression, and I might have been spared the necessity of fighting to get her the care she needed. Unfortunately, most hospice programs in the United States are home-based, because of Medicare incentives to keep spending down, according to Rhymes.

The Medicare Mess

Many experts agree, in fact, that Medicare rules contribute significantly to the problems hospice patients face. Hospices were born out of an altruistic ideal, but the Medicare hospice option was mainly created to save Medicare money by reducing hospitalizations and expensive life-saving attempts. According to Paul R. Torrens, a professor of public health at the University of California at Los Angeles, Medicare changed everything for hospice workers because they are now caught between helping the patient on the one hand and keeping costs down on the other. So when deciding not to give palliative surgical procedures, for example, hospice personnel may sometimes be guided more by economic pressures than by hospice philosophy. "Since the Medicare hospice benefit began, almost everything about hospice programs has had an economic flavor," says Torrens. "There are always economic pressures, though most hospice workers try to resist them."

Because of finances, some patients don't get complete care. "Hospice philosophy says the needs of each individual must dictate treatment, but many patients may not receive the best treatments due to financial restrictions," laments O'Connor. "Medicare limits a patient's options." For example, she notes, Medicare requires hospice patients to be treated at home at least 80 percent of the time and restricts how much hospices are allowed to spend on them. "Why should caregivers be allowed to spend only a fixed amount on care?" she asks. "Why should patients be required to sign a paper saying that their life expectancy is less than six months? Why should some hospice patients have to sign a 'do not resuscitate' order? These are invasions of privacy. To care effectively for the dying, we need flexibility, not all these rules and regulations."

Rigid Attitudes Toward Death

Of all the "rules" that can impinge on hospice patients, the most insidious may be the prescriptions about peaceful death. Some of Kübler-Ross's modern disciples have over-interpreted their mentor's theories about the "process" of dying to mean that there is one and only one right way to die. In my mother's case, for example, it was apparently "right" for her to calmly accept the news that she was supposed to die within six months, and to gasp for breath without expecting medical treatment because she was going to die soon anyway. . . .

Gorodezky believes that rigid attitudes are seen too often. "They're the result of oversimplified thinking," she says. "Kübler-Ross gave us a framework to understand the complexity of dying, but not a recipe. Patients have a right to die in their own way, and our only job as caregivers is to make them as comfortable as possible."

While admitting that he has heard of cases like my mother's "more than once," Bates emphasizes that hospices have improved tremendously in the past several years and keep getting better. And Rhymes insists that, whatever the flaws remaining in hospices, most experts believe they represent the best form of care available for the dying. The workers, she says, are generally warmer, more understanding and better trained than those who care for the dying in more traditional situations. But she admits that the training still needs to get considerably better. "There's still a lot we don't know about caring for the dying," she says. "There are still some things we need to learn about pain management, and still some symptoms we can't treat well."

"Most dying people are happier at home than in a hospital."

Home Care May Be Best for the Dying

Deborah Duda

Four out of five Americans die in hospitals, nursing homes, or other institutional settings. In the following viewpoint, Deborah Duda argues that spending their final days at home can be a much better alternative for dying patients. A comfortable, familiar environment and family support enables people to die with dignity and respect, she states. Duda is a writer who has been actively involved in death and dying issues. This viewpoint is excerpted from her book *Coming Home: A Guide to Dying at Home with Dignity*.

As you read, consider the following questions:

1. What is the importance of one's attitude toward death, according to Duda?
2. What guidelines does the author provide in making the decision to care for a dying person at home?
3. What fears do dying people have, according to Duda?

Reprinted from: *Coming Home: A Guide to Dying at Home with Dignity* by Deborah Duda, © 1987 Aurora Press. For further information about this and other titles, write to Aurora Press, PO Box 573, Santa Fe, NM 87504.

When we can no longer control the circumstances of our lives, we can still choose our attitude about them. We can choose our attitude about dying. We can choose to see it as a tragedy, teacher, adventure, or simply as an experience to be lived. Our *attitude* will determine the nature of our experience. An optimist and a pessimist see the same world, only through different lenses (attitudes). And as Norman Cousins said, "Pessimism is a waste of time. No one really knows enough to be a pessimist."

When we choose to surrender to life, we are free; and when we are free, we are in control. This paradox lies at the heart of our human existence. . . .

Hospital Death

As our Western culture emphasized control over nature, death became the uncontrollable enemy. We gave doctors the responsibility for combatting this enemy. Death became increasingly a medical "problem" instead of a natural event. We gave away the responsibility for death (and life) to experts outside of ourselves—big institutions and big business. Life-sustaining technology said a good death is a hospital death and an unobstructed natural death is euthanasia. And people seem to feel that because we invented machines, we have to use them. So life ends up not to be for living but to justify machinery. We have become medical consumers.

Ivan Illich, in his scholarly and intriguing history of our attitudes and practices about death, *Medical Nemesis*, calls death "the ultimate form of consumer resistance." Illich goes on to say, "Today the man best protected against setting the stage for his own dying is the sick person in critical condition. Society, acting through the medical system, decides when and after what indignities and mutilations he shall die." In the face of death we have felt powerless. This doesn't have to be. We're not dying to humour doctors by doing it *their* way or to make the medical community rich!

Taking Back Our Death

We have begun to take back what is rightfully ours—our life and our death. . . .

Once we gave the medical industry responsibility for our deaths, it became an act of personal courage to die at home. Now more and more courageous people are saying, "I don't want to go away to die. I want to die at home."

State and federal governments are financially supporting more home health care. Hospices that help care for our dying have developed all over the country. Insurance companies have added more home health care benefits to their services. Living

Wills that express how we wish to be treated when we're dying are becoming commonplace. Death and Dying Courses are taught in universities and medical schools across the country. Once again young doctors are recognizing the value of a family practice, personal care and house calls.

Regaining Personal Power

By taking responsibility for dying, we reclaim responsibility for living and regain the personal power we'd given away. One way to take responsibility is to stop playing victim to our culture's pressure to go away quietly and die in the sterility of a nursing home or hospital. Who wants to be seen as a forthcoming vacancy! We can die *right here* amidst the people and things we love, the kids, the dog, the garden, our favorite chair.

Deborah Duda, *Coming Home*, 1987.

We're returning to dying at home—the old natural way which most of the world never questioned.

We have a right to die with *dignity*. Dignity in the dictionary means "worthiness." To me it means doing things in our own way. Dying at home we maintain the ability to choose our own way, whether it be a little decision like what time we eat, or a big one like whether or not to use life-sustaining techniques.

We have a right to die with *respect*—to see and to be seen. At home a person remains an individual, rather than "the patient in Room 204B."

Dying at home, we can influence the quality and quantity of our lives.

Why Die at Home? The Advantages

(You may want to share this list with the dying person.)

1. Most dying people are happier at home than in a hospital.
2. The dying person can influence the quality and quantity of his or her own life.
3. Respect and dignity are maintained.
4. The dying person feels wanted.
5. You feel useful and needed.
6. The continued presence of love supports you both.
7. You both have more freedom and control. The dying person can tell you what he or she wants. (No one is awakened at 5:45 a.m. for temperature taking or the 20th blood sample.)
8. You both can live more normally and fully.
9. The dying person can teach you something about living.

10. Home is more supportive of the shift from *curing* to *making comfortable.*

11. In a familiar and secure outer environment, both of you have more time for the inner preparations for death.

12. There is time and a place to express feelings of grief, anger, and love, so accepting this death and death in general will be easier.

13. When physical death occurs, there's time to experience what's happened without the body being whisked away to make room for the next patient.

14. There's no travel wear and tear between home and hospital. (No worry about loved ones driving at night in bad weather.)

15. You both can see or create your own version of beauty.

16. Food at home can be fresher and more appetizing.

17. Living at home costs less.

18. Be it a slum or a palace, it's home!

I met a lovely 92-year-old Spanish lady in the hospital who sat in a wheelchair hooked to tubes, babbling, mostly incoherently, about her bedspread at home, the curtains and the good milk. It seemed to me she was still expressing what she wanted most—to be home. Home is a magic word.

When Is It Not Appropriate to Die at Home?

1. When the dying person doesn't want to.

2. When the family would be too upset to care for him or her.

3. When the hospital can provide services that improve the *quality* of a person's life.

4. When the dying person wants to be hooked into intravenous feedings (IVs), etc., and you can't afford a regular nurse.

5. When there is no one at home to care for the person and you can't afford to pay for someone.

6. It may not be appropriate if there are small children in the family who also need care; not because it wouldn't be good for them to be present, but because you might not be able to manage it all. (If you can't get sufficient extra help at home, a residential hospice program may be a solution.)

7. If the dying person plans to donate organs for transplant, the death needs to take place in a hospital because organs are transplanted soon after death.

Sometimes it's very clear-cut. The person who is dying says, "I want to die at home" or just, "I want to go home." If this happens, you, the family, can discuss among yourselves whether or not this choice will work for everyone concerned. Your preferences, as well as the dying person's, need to be considered. The decision to come home must be a joint one. *Only a family that wants someone to come home can give the care needed.*

More often the situation is not so clear. The sick person still may hope to get better and may well do so. Or, someone may not know or want to know how sick she or he is, and feel anxious, afraid and confused. And family and friends may feel the same. It's hard to feel clear about dying when we're getting a morass of conflicting reports from different parts of ourselves; body, mind, feelings and soul each report their own story or reality. . . .

Give loving support and information to help everyone involved make the best decision possible at this time. Include in the information what you *want* to do, finances, your own state of health, child care and the availability of help. To avoid total exhaustion, *I recommend there be at least two people at home to take turns supporting the dying person.* . . .

Probably you'll want to discuss the choices with a doctor. Remember, a doctor in this circumstance is a provider of information, not a decision-maker. Usually, she or he is accustomed to recommending the hospital for very sick people. If a hospital is recommended, ask how it can serve the dying person besides prolonging life. . . .

Respect Your Feelings

A decision need not be permanent. If a person is at home and you still have doubts or it's not working out, a hospital, hospice or nursing home is always available. Returning someone can be emotionally difficult for all concerned, and sometimes it's necessary. Respect your feelings. *You are just as valuable as the dying person.*

Examine your motives carefully before bringing someone home. If guilt is the motive ("If I were a good person, I'd bring her home" or "I *should* bring him home"), you probably won't have the energy to keep going until the person dies. Love sustains us; guilt drains us. . . .

Pain management is one of the great fears of the dying and their families. *In most cases pain can be alleviated just as well at home as in the hospital.* In my experience dying people living at home have less pain than those in a hospital. Love is a very effective stress and pain reducer. If the dying person cannot take pills or liquids, a nurse can give injections or you can learn to give them yourself. With a nurse's help even IVs can come home. *Pain control isn't something to fear; just something to do.*

Another fear of a dying person is, "What will happen to my family?" When he or she sees you at home coping and handling well this terminal illness, the fear will be alleviated. At home there's time for making the appropriate arrangements.

Dying people also fear being a burden. Reassure them they're not and that their dying is part of the whole family's life. For example, when I suggested coming home while Dad was dying, Mom said, "But you've got to get on with your life, Deborah." My response was, "What happens in my family is part of my life." You might say to someone who wants to be at home but who fears being a burden, "Allowing ourselves to receive love and caring is just as important as giving them. Please let us return some of the love you've given to us by allowing us to care for you at home." Or to a real stubborn person, "Are you going to give the pleasure and privilege of caring for you to your family or to strangers?"

Familiar Surroundings

In years past, most people died at home. That is still a possibility. Many people prefer the idea of dying in familiar, comfortable surroundings instead of a hospital. At home, dying persons can still maintain some control over their lives; in a hospital, they may feel that their schedule is determined by others.

If your loved one prefers to remain at home, ask your doctor to recommend in-home medical services. You and other members of your family may need training on how to care for your loved one. Although caring for a dying person can be strenuous, you may later treasure this time you could spend together.

National Funeral Directors Association, *Living with Dying*, 1987.

Dying people, as well as a lot of the rest of us, fear loneliness and being deserted. In Malcolm Muggeridge's *Something Beautiful for God*, Mother Teresa says:

I have come more and more to realize that it is being unwanted that is the worst disease that any human being can ever experience. . . . For all kinds of diseases there are medicines and cures. But for being unwanted, except there are willing hands to serve and there's a loving heart to love, I don't think this terrible disease can ever be cured.

Bringing dying people home reassures them they're wanted and won't be deserted. And we may have to reassure them many times. Being at home also alleviates loneliness.

Dying people fear losing control over their lives. In the hospital, the staff takes over and largely dictates what the patient can and must do, when you can see them, etc. You and the dying person don't have time to adjust *gradually* to loss of control. At home, on the other hand, you can take a few steps at a time toward giving up control which makes dying easier.

The feeling of being totally wrenched by an unnatural catastrophe, common in sudden deaths and many hospital deaths, is less likely to occur at home. You know you're doing all you can do. If the thought comes up afterward, "Maybe I could have done more," you're likely to let go of it much more quickly than if you'd been isolated from a loved one in a hospital. After caring for someone who dies at home most people report feeling peace as well as loss—a feeling of appropriateness and completion and a greater openness to the new life ahead. Mom said, "I feel good because Dad was so happy to be at home and die the way he wanted to."

Sometimes the dying person is medically termed 'unconscious' and has earlier expressed a desire to be home or has signed a "living will." A living will is a document we can sign any time in our adult lives instructing doctors to withhold or withdraw extraordinary life sustaining procedures during a terminal illness.

Patients whose level of consciousness is uncertain may still let us know what they want. You can ask, for example, "Do you want to go home? Squeeze my hand for 'yes'—blink for 'no'." Use whatever signal you can invent using the abilities the person still has available.

A Legal Right

Few people realize *we have the legal right to leave a hospital whenever we please*, with or without a doctor's approval. A family has the legal right to make a decision for a person who is "incompetent," not able to make or express his or her own decisions. Under these circumstances, the next of kin can take responsibility for checking the patient out of the hospital. You may have to sign a form stating that the patient is leaving the hospital "against medical advice." Attending physicians most frequently just drop a case if they don't agree, but they can resort to legal proceedings if they feel it's not in the best interest of the patient to leave. This is uncommon.

Hopefully you will have no difficulty in bringing a loved one home from the hospital. Most states have recently passed Living Will Laws which legally protect our right to refuse treatment. The American Hospital Association has drawn up a Patient's Bill of Rights which also affirms this right. . . .

Once you've made the decision for home, keep in mind that your focus shifts from *curing* to *making comfortable*. Now, do everything possible for comfort rather than to prolong life, as long as the dying person is in agreement. A dying person may want to prolong life for some reason . . . seeing a son or daughter graduate from school, a grandchild born, etc. People have a right to change their decisions.

"By constantly seeking to minimize the endemic 'depersonalization' of the [hospital] institution, hospice staff can serve as a model for the institution."

Hospitals Can Effectively Respond to the Dying

Ina Ajemian and Balfour Mount

After being criticized for being insensitive to dying patients, some hospitals have developed special units, modeled after the hospice concept, to care for the dying. The authors of the following viewpoint, Ina Ajemian and Balfour Mount, developed one of the first hospice units within a hospital. In the following viewpoint, they describe the unit, called the Palliative Care Service, located at the Royal Victoria Hospital in Montreal, Canada. By combining hospice and hospital, patients get both excellent palliative care (care designed to relieve pain) and the comprehensive service and technology hospitals have to offer. Ajemian is director of the Palliative Care Service at Royal Victorian Hospital. Mount is professor of surgery and director of palliative care medicine at McGill University in Montreal, Canada.

As you read, consider the following questions:

1. What are some of the goals the authors describe of hospice/ palliative care units in hospitals?
2. How do hospice units benefit hospitals, according to Ajemian and Mount?
3. How do the authors say hospice units in hospitals benefit dying patients?

From *The Hospice: Development and Administration*, 2d ed., Glen W. Davidson, ed., © 1985. With permission from Hemisphere Publishing Corporation, New York & Washington, D.C.

During the last decade, two facts have become evident: the care of the terminally ill has been grossly deficient in our modern health care system, and their needs can be met more effectively with special services designed to complement services in the traditional health care system. With 70 percent of today's patients dying in institutions, the extent of these problems cannot be minimized.

The hundreds of hospice/palliative care programs established in the last ten years in response to this challenge have a number of factors which depart from the traditional mode.

• Whole person care is mandatory. Excellence in pain and symptom control is the foundation for emphasis on psychological, social and spiritual issues.

• Both patients and their families are considered in setting goals of care.

• Bereavement support for key family members is considered to be an integral part of comprehensive terminal care programs.

• Every effort is made in an inpatient setting to minimize "institutional depersonalization" and to foster individuality, informality and a home-like lifestyle.

• Although the uncertainty of prognosis is recognized, terminal care is "life oriented," focusing on the control of symptoms which permits enhanced relationships, reconciliation, sense of fulfillment and personal growth.

• New models of interdisciplinary teams are required to meet such a broad problem mandate, necessitating the development of new patterns of interaction and the inclusion of effective support mechanisms.

The Need for Specialized Care

The Palliative Care Service of the Royal Victoria Hospital represents one attempt to adapt these principles to the needs of a thousand-bed teaching hospital community. The service was instituted in 1975, following a study which underlined the great deficiencies in care of dying patients throughout the hospital. The service consists of an eighteen-bed inpatient unit, hospital-based home care, a consultation/symptom control team which visits patients throughout the hospital, an outpatient clinic and bereavement follow-up care. . . .

In a time of major economic constraint, it is important to ask whether the development of yet another specialized service for patient care is warranted. Is it not possible to train all hospital and home care staff to give improved terminal care? While educational programs in death and dying have increased staff awareness of the particular needs of terminally ill patients and their families, there remains a basic problem: the discrepancy between the orientation of hospitals and the needs of these patients. The training and skills of professional staff in general hospitals are focused toward four ends: investigation, diagnosis, cure and prolongation of life. These activities are largely irrelevant to terminally ill patients—for whom quality of life is the only appropriate goal. . . .

A Hospice Unit in a General Hospital

When, as often happens, the transition from active anti-cancer therapy to palliative care is unclear, difficult or delayed, the presence of the palliative care team within the institution facilitates early involvement, and lessens the trauma attached to the shift in therapeutic goals. In a hospice unit attached to a hospital, resources, such as skilled personnel and specialized equipment (for example, consultant neurologists and radiation therapists), are readily available when needed for symptom alleviation.

Changes in Traditional Care

The non-hospice programmes of care, the traditional doctor in hospital and nursing home programmes of care which many of us despaired of for so long, . . . are now beginning to undergo change and metamorphosis on the basis of what they have seen and learned in hospice systems. On all sides in southern California I see the traditional programmes of care for dying patients in traditional hospitals with traditional doctors now being expanded and having particular services added to them that were simply not there before—a nurse, a social worker, a counsellor, home care services, transportation or even day hospitals. . . .

That may perhaps be the most significant achievement of all: that the development of hospice programmes has brought about quietly and gradually, but significantly, an improvement and upgrading of the programmes of the care for the dying in the standard, traditional or conventional settings where, in fact, most people die.

Paul Torrens, in *Hospice: The Living Idea*, 1981.

The physical proximity of hospice and acute care units may stimulate improved care in both areas. All too often, as documented by Raymond Duff and August Hollingshead, hospitalization involves a series of dehumanizing events serving to incorporate patients into the procedures of the institution and eventually eliminating all sense of autonomy, identity and status as individuals. The hospice focus on whole person medicine serves as a reminder to the institution at large that patients are unique individuals whose suffering may involve many aspects of their personhood. By constantly seeking to minimize the endemic "depersonalization" of the institution, hospice staff can serve as a model for the institution. Questions of appropriate therapy, when the potential for cure or prolongation of life is slight, are often difficult. Hospice staff, as advocates for patients in their total contexts—physical, social and emotional—can insure that decisions reflect anticipated benefits, weighed against anticipated morbidity in all these spheres. Furthermore, the close liaison between acute care wards and a hospice insures medical peer review of the hospice and provides an inherent accountability. The concern with insuring a high standard of medical competence in the hospice team is thus less problematic in this setting than in a hospice physically separated, and without close affiliation, to a medical center.

Patients and their families may experience an enhanced sense of security and trust if continuing concern is demonstrated in the primary treating institution through the provision of a range of services spanning the whole period from initial diagnosis to bereavement follow-up.

One other advantage of a hospice within a hospital environment is cost. In many parts of North America there is currently underutilization of hospital beds. The location of hospices in general hospitals avoids many of the costs related to the development of a new facility. In addition, such a unit can maximize the efficiency of utilizing existing inpatient beds. . . .

Hospice Consultation Team in a General Hospital

This type of hospice unit provides service for palliative care patients who are inappropriate for transfer or do not wish to be transferred to hospice units. It may be useful to patients facing death in a variety of hospital settings (for example, oncology or intensive care units, or emergency departments).

Hospice consultation teams may be easier to introduce than hospice units in hospital settings in which space and resources are limited. These teams, working alongside staff throughout the hospitals, can do a great deal to change attitudes toward the terminally ill and their families and improve the skill of staff generally. Team members frequently serve as advocates for patients with hospital staff and administrations. . . .

The goals of the Palliative Care Service are the relief of suffering and the enhancement of life. . . .

Certain principles will guide hospice staff in their attempts to diminish the suffering of patients.

Diagnostic and therapeutic goals must be set in terms of the patients and not their diseases. For example, prolonged courses of radiotherapy which change the ultimate prognosis very little cannot be justified since they may simply be increasing discomfort, fears, length of hospital stays and costs. On the other hand, prompt radiotherapy in spinal cord compression, for example, may avert paraplegia, thus preventing a blow to independent functioning. Blood transfusion rarely improves the quality of life for bed-bound patients, but may enable an ambulatory patient to function more fully. To choose which therapy is appropriate requires considerable knowledge of the particular patient, the particular disease, and the particular situation.

Hospitals Have Improved

If you or someone you care for is facing death in a hospital setting, you may find that the situation has improved over the last few years. Recently there has been an increase in the number of medical professionals with an awareness of the special needs of the dying. Health care administrator Jeanne Benoliel points out that over the last decade a general move toward death awareness has "legitimized medical care of the dying patient and permitted the introduction of palliative care services and hospice units into established hospitals. It stimulated a variety of workshops and other educational activities to prepare physicians, nurses, and other health care providers for work that involved them with dying patients and their families.". . .

Today's hospital staff may be more attentive and helpful toward a patient who is dying, even though they are not trained to provide death care.

In today's hospital you are much more likely to find what is called a "palliative care" or "comfort care" unit where patients at the end stages of terminal disease can receive pain management and emotional support instead of curative treatment. Many medical professionals are truly interested in trying to assist, rather than deny or ignore, the dying process. Their experiences have sensitized them to the need for providing comfort and care rather than inappropriately aggressive treatment.

Patricia Anderson, *Affairs in Order*, 1991.

All efforts should be made to maximize patients' functions and not their length of life. This frequently implies reducing hospital stays to a minimum, and teaching families to provide care. It may require taking some risks, such as allowing ambulation where the possibility of pathological fracture exists or using nonsteroidal anti-inflammatory drugs and steroids for pain relief and to provide enhanced patient well-being even if there is a risk of perforating ulcer.

Every effort should be made to actively minimize suffering. This requires that competent physicians exercise skill in correctly diagnosing the physiological mechanism underlying patients' physical symptoms, and in manipulating the various drug and other treatment modalities to achieve relief. There is no place in the hospice concept for substandard medical care.

As every aspect of personhood—physical, emotional, social and spiritual—may suffer loss and injury, hospice staff must be prepared to intervene in any aspect. Their relationships with patients and their knowledge of the personhood of each provides the vehicle for diagnosing suffering and intervening effectively. . . .

Patients as Team Members

Patients and key persons (families and others at significant risk in bereavement) are integral members of the health care team on the PCU. This fact is symbolic of the differences in direction between palliative and acute care wards. The significance of their inclusion on the team lies not only in the need to consult and obtain active input from them in drawing up the plan of care, but also in the need to include them as "caregivers" (and not just receivers) to the extent they wish. Such a policy serves to counter the institutional depersonalization many of these patients have experienced. It also assists the key persons in their anticipatory grief.

Distinguishing Between Fact and Opinion

This activity is designed to help develop the basic reading and thinking skill of distinguishing between fact and opinion. Consider the following statement as an example: "There are more than fifteen hundred hospices in the United States." This is a factual statement which could be verified by checking with such organizations as the National Hospice Organization. But the statement "Hospices provide better care for dying patients than hospitals" is an opinion. Some people believe that hospitals, with their greater medical resources, are equal or better than hospices at providing treatment for the dying.

When investigating controversial issues it is important that one be able to distinguish between statements of fact and statements of opinion. It is also important to recognize that not all statements of fact are true. They may appear to be true, but some are based on inaccurate or false information. For this activity, however, we are concerned with understanding the difference between those statements that appear to be factual and those that appear to be based primarily on opinion.

Most of the following statements are taken from the viewpoints in this chapter. Consider each statement carefully. *Mark O for any statement you believe is an opinion or interpretation of facts. Mark F for any statement you believe is a fact. Mark I for any statement you believe is impossible to judge.*

If you are doing this activity as a member of a class or group, compare your answers with those of other class or group members. Be able to defend your answers. You may discover that others come to different conclusions than you do. Listening to the reasons others present for their answers may give you valuable insights into distinguishing between fact and opinion.

O = opinion
F = fact
I = impossible to judge

95

1. According to the National Hospice Census, there are about two hundred thousand patients being served by hospices.

2. The most successful model for enlightened death care today is the hospice.

3. Most hospices in the United States are not housed in separate buildings or institutions, but are instead support networks for caring for the dying at home.

4. Hospitals should improve their pain-management procedures when dealing with dying patients.

5. Under federal law, Medicare-funded hospices must have a physician determine that a prospective patient is not expected to live more than six months.

6. Many of the problems of hospice treatment result from Medicare rules.

7. The official goals of hospices are comfort and patient support.

8. Hospices are very successful in meeting their goals of comfort and patient support.

9. Many hospice workers believe there is only one right way to die.

10. The principles of hospice care as defined by the National Hospice Organization state that the family members are extremely important in caring for the dying.

11. Hospices have improved tremendously in the past few years.

12. Studies of terminally ill patients reveal that as many as 50 percent do not suffer from pain at all.

13. Many hospices care for the dying in teams, which consist of a physician, nurses, counselors, and volunteers.

14. We have a right to die with dignity.

15. Until the past few decades, most people died at home.

16. The home is a more comfortable environment than a hospital.

17. People must learn to accept death.

18. When we are dying we need support, warmth, and compassion.

Periodical Bibliography

The following articles have been selected to supplement the diverse views presented in this chapter.

James N. Baker	"A Gentle Place to Live and Die," *Newsweek,* July 29, 1991.
Cynthia B. and Peter J. Cohen	"Do-Not-Resuscitate Orders in the Operating Room," *The New England Journal of Medicine,* December 26, 1991. Available from 10 Shattuck St., Boston, MA 02115-6094.
Mark A. Duntley Jr.	"Covenantal Ethics and Care for the Dying," *The Christian Century,* December 4, 1991.
Kirsti A. Dyer	"Reshaping Our Views of Death and Dying," *Journal of the American Medical Association,* March 4, 1992. Available from the American Medical Association, 515 N. State St., Chicago, IL 60610.
Holly Fleischman	"Criticisms of Hospice," *Free Inquiry,* Winter 1991/1992. Available from PO Box 664, Buffalo, NY 14226-0664.
Stephen Levine	"Conscious Dying," *Utne Reader,* September/October 1991.
Andrew H. Malcolm	"The Ultimate Decision," *The New York Times Magazine,* December 3, 1989.
Bonnie J. Miller-McLemore	"Doing Wrong, Getting Sick, and Dying," *The Christian Century,* February 24, 1988.
William E. Phipps	"Health Technology vs. Death: Should We Prolong the Inevitable?" *USA Today,* January 1989.
Vernon Pizer	"Hospices: the Final Pilgrimage," *The American Legion,* July 1988.
Jill Rhymes	"Hospice Care in America," *Journal of the American Medical Association,* July 18, 1990.
Kurt Rosenberg	"Musically Midwifing Death," *Utne Reader,* September/October 1991.
Cicely Saunders	"The Evolution of the Hospices," *Free Inquiry,* Winter 1991/1992.
Beth Spring	"A Genuinely 'Good Death,'" *Christianity Today,* July 15, 1988.
William C. Wilson et al.	"Ordering and Administering of Sedatives and Analgesics During the Withholding and Withdrawal of Life Support from Critically Ill Patients," *Journal of the American Medical Association,* February 19, 1992.

How Can Dying Patients Control the Decision to End Treatment?

DEATH̶DYING

Chapter Preface

Many people fear the prospect of being kept alive by medical technology beyond the point of meaningful existence. Professor of religion William E. Phipps calls this prospect "postmature death" and argues that as technology advances and enables physicians to extend the lives of very ill patients, an increasing number of Americans may face it. Phipps describes the case of a seventy-five-year-old man whose brain was irreparably damaged after he suffered heart failure, but who was kept alive on a respirator for an additional month. The man's daughter stated:

> My handsome, energetic father, a man who always took great pride in his appearance, lay on a hospital bed paralyzed from the neck down. There were tubes running in and tubes running out. His nostrils were taped back and open. . . . For the elderly who are totally incapacitated, there comes a time to call it quits. . . . There was nothing uglier than the fashion in which my father was forced to die.

While patients have the legal right to refuse medical treatment, many, such as the man described above, are incapacitated and unable to communicate their wishes. To prevent such situations, some people advocate communicating wishes concerning treatment before a crisis occurs. The best-known method of doing this is the living will, a legal document in which a person can direct against "extraordinary" measures in the event of irreversible coma or terminal illness.

Despite the fact that 90 percent of people polled say they do not wish to be kept on artificial life-support systems if there is no hope of recovery, fewer than 15 percent of Americans have made out living wills. The 1991 Patient Self-Determination Act attempts to encourage their use by requiring medical institutions to ask incoming patients if they have advance directives or wish to complete one. Whether or not the act will encourage Americans to make and sign living wills remains to be seen.

Debates remain on what kind of written directives are best, whether such written notices can fully anticipate all of a dying patient's circumstances, and whether written directives may cause more harm than good to the dying patient. The viewpoints in this chapter explore these issues.

"A duly executed will and a law can permit physicians, hospitals and nursing homes to honor a person's desires without legal repercussions."

Living Wills Can Best Enable Patients to End Treatment

Jane E. Brody

A living will is a written directive in which a person expresses his or her wishes to have life-sustaining treatment withheld in the event of terminal illness. In the following viewpoint, Jane E. Brody describes how her mother-in-law's living will enabled her to die peacefully and with dignity. Brody argues that living wills are valuable because they allow people control over what kind of treatment they wish to receive, and thus avoid the prospect of lengthy, lingering deaths prolonged by modern medicine. Brody is an award-winning science writer and personal health columnist for the *New York Times*.

As you read, consider the following questions:

1. What comparisons does Brody make between the deaths of her mother and mother-in-law?
2. How many Americans have living wills, according to the author?
3. How can a person obtain and write out a living will, according to Brody?

In June 1989, four years after she was first treated for cancer, my mother-in-law made out a "living will," specifying her desire not to be given any means of life support should she become terminally ill or permanently unconscious.

Her act was a little late—she was 84 years old at the time—but not too late. Just two months after she had signed the will before two witnesses, she was hospitalized with intestinal bleeding. Fully believing that her cancer had recurred, she told the staff at her hospital that she did not want surgery, transfusions or feeding tubes. She just wanted to be allowed to die as peacefully and comfortably as possible.

The hospital posted a "Do Not Resuscitate" notice on her chart and told her and the gathering family what to expect. Staff members assured everyone they would provide medication to minimize her pain.

Twelve hours later, after saying calm goodbyes to three generations of relatives and dozens of friends, she slipped quietly into a coma and her heart and breathing stopped.

A Living Will

A living will, which specifies exactly which forms of treatment should be rejected or applied, is not usually invoked unless the patient is unable to communicate a refusal of life support. But the fact that my mother-in-law had signed one kept family, friends and medical personnel from trying to persuade her to fight to stay alive with any weapon medicine could offer.

As a result, she died painlessly and with dignity, without undue physical or emotional suffering for herself or those who loved her. Unfortunately, few deaths these days are so peaceful and unencumbered by the medical trappings that so often distance the dying from those who care.

Although more than 30 years have passed since my own mother died of cancer, I have never forgotten or recovered from the terror I experienced in her last hours as tubes and machines sustained a shell of a person toward no meaningful end.

Ways of Sustaining Life

It can be much worse today. Every hospital can now maintain a person's breathing, circulation and nutrition long after the body has lost its ability to perform these life-sustaining tasks. And unless the patient, in writing or through a designated surrogate, specifies a desire not to be kept alive by artificial means when there is no hope for recovery, the doctor and hospital usually feel obliged to do whatever they can to sustain life.

It is a costly obligation, not just in terms of money spent on medical care but also in the emotional suffering of those close to the patient.

Yet, only 9 percent of Americans have executed a living will to assure that their wishes regarding medical treatment during terminal illness will be honored even if they become comatose or mentally incompetent.

The living will has been accepted as ethical by most religions and medical organizations, including the American Medical Association. In a survey of physicians conducted for the Association, 78 percent of the respondents said they favored withdrawing life support from hopelessly ill or irreversibly comatose patients if they or their families request it.

A Sample Living Will

To my family, my physicians, my lawyer, and all others whom it may concern:

If the time comes when I can no longer take part in decisions for my own future, let this statement stand as an expression of my wishes and directions, while I am still of sound mind.

If at such a time the situation should arise in which there is no reasonable expectation of my recovery from extreme physical or mental disability, I direct that I be allowed to die and not be kept alive by medications, artificial means or "heroic measures." I do, however, ask that medication be mercifully administered to me to alleviate suffering even though this may shorten my remaining life.

This statement is made after careful consideration and is in accordance with my strong convictions and beliefs. I want the wishes and directions here expressed carried out to the extent permitted by law. Insofar as they are not legally enforceable, I hope that those to whom this Will is addressed will regard themselves as morally bound by these provisions.

Signed _____ Date _____

Witness _____

Witness _____

Copies of this request have been given to _____

_____

Dying with Dignity, *I Don't Know What to Say*, 1988.

Moreover, hospitals seeking accreditation now must establish formal policies on how to handle patients who do not want to be resuscitated.

But, as 12 physicians writing in *The New England Journal of Medicine* said, there is a large gap between acceptance of the concept of a living will and its implementation. Few physicians, they said, discuss such matters with their patients.

The authors, who represent a variety of medical specialties, had participated in a conference on hopelessly ill patients. In their special article they urged physicians to initiate timely discussions with patients about life-sustaining treatment and terminal care. They also urged hospitals, health maintenance organizations and nursing homes to ask patients upon admission whether they have prepared a living will or designated someone to act in their behalf in making medical decisions.

Legal Status

Through a living will, you can ask not to be resuscitated if your breathing has stopped, and can specify the conditions under which a "Do Not Resuscitate" order should be placed on your medical chart. Such an order can also be requested orally or, if you are not able to make such a request, it can be done by a medical surrogate or a family member.

The first living-will law took effect in California in 1976. Forty states and the District of Columbia now have legislation recognizing the legality of such wills. In several other states, including New York and New Jersey, court decisions have affirmed the legality of such wills.

In addition, laws or judicial opinions in 17 states have affirmed the person to designate someone to make decisions about medical matters should the person be unable to do so.

Fenella Rouse, acting director of the Society for the Right to Die, an advocacy group, said laws and court decisions merely spelled out what was already accepted practice.

"No medical institution or physician has ever been sued successfully for stopping life support consistent with a patient's wishes, even if the patient had no living will," she said. But a duly executed will and a law can permit physicians, hospitals and nursing homes to honor a person's desires without legal repercussions.

And a living will is not forever binding; it can be amended or revoked to reflect changes in your thinking.

Forms Available

The laws and court-sanctioned actions governing living wills now form a crazy quilt throughout the country. Accordingly, the Society for the Right to Die has prepared different forms that comply with the laws in every state. . . .

In New York State, for example, a living will would apply to a person "in an incurable or irreversible mental or physical condition with no reasonable expectation of recovery."

The conditions of the will would be put into effect if the person is in a terminal condition, permanently unconscious, or conscious but with irreversible brain damage.

There is also space on each will for more specific instructions. For example, a person with AIDS or advanced cancer may specify that he does not want treatment other than to relieve pain and anxiety should he develop life-threatening complications.

Living wills must be signed, dated and countersigned by two witnesses—ideally, not relatives who may become heirs. Make several copies of the completed document and keep the original with your important personal papers, but not in a safety deposit box because no one else can get to it. Give a copy to your physician to include in your medical records, another copy to your closest relative or friend and a third to your attorney.

The Society for the Right to Die also urges each person to assign "durable power of attorney for medical treatment" to a close relative or friend who can make decisions for you should you be unable to decide for yourself about any aspect of care that may not be covered in the living will.

> *"I am sure you have heard those who would defend the notion that a 'Living Will'. . . will protect the individual from being subjected to cruel and unwanted treatment. . . . Not so."*

Living Wills Do Not Ensure a Patient's Right to Die

Lauraine Thomas

The living will has been touted as a way to prevent receiving unwanted medical treatment during a terminal illness. In the following viewpoint, Lauraine Thomas argues that living wills do not achieve their desired goal because they are too easily ignored by physicians. Doctors, she asserts, often arbitrarily overrule living wills and impose unwanted medical treatment. Thomas is a nurse and educator on health issues.

As you read, consider the following questions:

1. What is tragic about modern dying, according to Thomas?
2. How do some physicians bypass living wills, according to the author?
3. How does Thomas compare doctors' and nurses' experiences and attitudes toward dying patients?

Lauraine Thomas, "Living Will Could Let You Down," *Hemlock Quarterly*, January 1992. Reprinted with permission.

After many years in the health care field as a critical care nurse and instructor to health care professionals (including physicians), I have witnessed time and again the arbitrary decisions made by physicians who consider themselves the sole legitimate judges of moral and ethical standards in health care.

The tragic consequences of such arrogance are evident everywhere, particularly in situations where the patient has made clear a desire to shorten the dying process by refusing treatment but is overruled by the physician whose personal code of ethics is imposed on the patient. This forces the patient to suffer the agony of prolonged dying and finally succumb to overwhelming failure of vital organ systems.

Doubly tragic is that the patient's suffering can be prolonged indefinitely due to the increasing sophistication of technology available to health care professionals.

The Weakness of Living Wills

I am sure you have heard those who would defend the notion that a "Living Will" or "Power of Attorney for Health Care" will protect the individual from being subjected to cruel and unwanted treatment by physicians whose arbitrary decisions are diametrically opposed to the patient's wishes. Not so.

Here is why: (and, I wish every person could understand the underlying weaknesses in both of these documents!) the attending physician simply can declare that the patient is suffering from "impaired mental status" and therefore is not competent to decide what is best for him or her—that the patient might after all, wish to "change his or her mind" about the provisions in the "Living Will"—but is unable due to "impaired mental status."

As defined by physicians, "impaired mental status" is so broad that it can be due to the patient having received pain-killing drugs, or has even a modest electrolyte imbalance, or suffers intractable pain, or that old standby, the patient is depressed.

Just about any excuse is sufficient reason to deny the patient's pleas for an end to suffering. Somehow physicians cannot bring themselves to look upon an individual's perfectly normal reaction to the hopelessness of life and suffering as permissible.

The notion that the patient is safeguarded by medical ethics that require a similar diagnosis and opinion by two or three "uninvolved" physicians or medical experts is at once naive and tragic. The fact is that such "consultations" are extraordinarily easy to come by.

There is much truth in the concept of an "old boys club" among physicians. I have yet to know of ANY consulting physician disagreeing with any other physician who requests such a consultation. The motions are gone through and the outcome always is the same—total agreement with the attending physician.

After all, someday the consulting physicians may wish agreement from the attending physician to confirm a diagnosis of "mental impairment" in order to impose their morality on a patient!

As for the "Power of Attorney for Health Care"—a perfectly legal and noble effort by the patient to place his or her fate in the hands of a trusted spouse, family member or friend—it too can fail to protect the patient.

Drawbacks of Living Wills

Living wills have significant drawbacks. First, a will drafted in specific language cannot provide guidance for circumstances that were not anticipated when the will was written. If, on the other hand, the will is written in general language to cover a broad range of possible circumstances, then its terms may be ambiguous in particular situations. In addition, many statutes restrict the kinds of directions that may be given in a living will. For example, living will statutes often apply only in the setting of a "terminal condition," which is generally defined as an irreversible condition that makes death imminent. A living will statute, then, may not apply if the patient suffers from a persistent vegetative state. Moreover, in some states, the living will statute may not apply to the withdrawal of a feeding tube.

David Orentlicher, *JAMA*, May 2, 1990.

Here is why: unless the entrusted person is extremely knowledgeable about those actions that can be taken any hour of the day or night by physicians, nurses, EMTs [Emergency Medical Technicians], etc., and literally can act as "bodyguard" to see that unwanted treatments are not forced upon the patient, such treatments may indeed be undertaken anyway.

Let me give an example: the patient does not wish to have dying prolonged by "extraordinary measures" (a splendidly vague term). During the night, in the absence of this trusted "bodyguard" the patient experiences a sudden difficulty in breathing. An intern or resident is notified by the nurse. The patient is intubated and placed on a ventilator in spite of protests against such action.

The intern or resident reasons that, due to the patient's difficult breathing, he or she is suffering from anoxia and the brain is not functioning normally due to reduced cerebral oxygen flow. Ergo, he or she has "impaired mental status" and the physician is free to undertake whatever is required to relieve the anoxia.

Never mind that the patient may indeed become ventilator-dependent, unable ever to breathe unaided again, and may suffer further physiologic insults of pneumonia, rampant fungus infection, and the agony of being unable to speak.

Legal Obstacles

Once in place, the ventilator becomes a "legal obstacle" to the patient's wishes. That is, to remove it could place the physician, hospital, et al., in jeopardy for having discontinued a "life-sustaining" treatment. The die is cast. The patient is condemned to a prolonged, agonizing dying process he or she desperately wished to avoid.

In this day and age, the application of a ventilator is not considered an "extra-ordinary measure" and the trusted "Attorney for Health Care" will be powerless to do anything about it short of undertaking an enormously costly and tedious battle through the courts to obtain a court order to discontinue "life-sustaining" measures in place—never granted short of "brain-death."

The patient is condemned to submit to all the painful and terrifying procedures that accompany the maintenance of a ventilator. Worse yet, "impaired mental status" can forever be claimed based on the presence of the ventilator.

There is one way that MAY help (but surely cannot guarantee) that such a scenario would not take place for this example patient. If the patient's trusted "Attorney for Health Care" was knowledgeable enough to list PRECISELY each and every treatment that would be forbidden in the care of the patient at the time of the patient's admission to the hospital, there is a better chance that the patient would not be subjected to them.

However, the admitting or attending physician or the hospital would be unlikely to agree to such prohibitions since, once again, each fears litigation for "inadequate patient care."

Avoid Hospitals

There is a moral here—if one wishes to know that his or her wishes will be honored no matter what subsequent developments may occur, one should avoid hospitalization. At the present time, I see very few options until the so-called "ethicists" (self-appointed judges of public morals) and those who deliver health care can give up the notion that they know what is "best" for the rest of us ordinary mortals and understand that there is only ONE person who knows what is best for the individual—the individual. That, to my mind, is an absolute.

Each individual must be permitted to make ALL decisions about his or her life (and death) as he or she ALONE sees fit. NO ONE should be permitted to inflict morality upon another person. NO ONE should have the power to overrule the decisions of the individual about his or her own well being, particularly when it comes to choosing the moment of death. In my

108

judgement, every individual should be permitted to end his or her life at a moment of his or her choosing.

Moreover, in my judgement, the greatest compassion that could be shown by those of us in the health care arena is not simply to stand by, but to actively assist the individual through a painless end to a life that, judged by the individual alone, has become too painful or too miserable to endure further.

The Need for Euthanasia

In short, I am among those who strongly believe in euthanasia in its truest sense—the good death. A great many of my nurse colleagues join me privately if not publicly in this belief, for it is the nurses who are constantly at the bedside of the suffering patient denied a good death.

The physician is spared dealing with the patient's agony 24 hours a day and confines his attention to ten minute visits perhaps a couple of times a day, most of which is spent reading the patient's chart.

Until the day comes when euthanasia—the good death—becomes every individual's right—when such compassion can be extended without fear of reprisals by courts, etc., publications such as *Final Exit* and organizations such as the Hemlock Society fulfill a desperate need.

"You don't need a Living Will, . . . you need trust in your doctor and family."

Living Wills Can Lead to Unnecessary Deaths

Raymond Voulo

Raymond Voulo is a physician in private practice in Port Washington, New York. In the following viewpoint, he argues that living wills are dangerous because they can legally prevent doctors from providing food, water, and medical treatment that might save patients' lives. He states that patients have the right to refuse unwanted medical treatment without writing living wills. Voulo concludes that living wills may eventually lead to the practice and acceptance of euthanasia, which he strongly opposes.

As you read, consider the following questions:

1. What phrases in a sample living will does Voulo find vague and objectionable?
2. Why does the author object to the removal of food and fluids from a patient?
3. Why do people sign living wills, according to Voulo?

Adapted from the January 1991 A.L.L. pamphlet *The "Living Will" and Euthanasia* by Raymond Voulo. Copyright 1991 by the American Life League. Reprinted with permission.

Recently, while reminiscing about the "good old days" of what once was called the art of the practice of medicine, I remembered how, in contrast to today, patients trusted their doctors enough to seek guidance on difficult questions concerning medical treatment.

Longing for those times, I envisioned the following exchange between myself and an imaginary patient "Joe" concerning the burning issues of the "Living Will" and euthanasia. I imagined Joe's questions and my answers as follows:

Doc, what's this Living Will that I've been hearing so much about lately?

Dangerous Language

Joe, the Living Will is a legal document which would prevent me, under civil penalty, from using "artificial means" to keep you alive in the event of certain illnesses. Since it is a legal document, Joe, every word in it has significance. Allow me to read to you part of a sample Living Will: "If I am permanently unconscious or there is no reasonable expectation of my recovery from a seriously incapacitating or lethal illness or condition, I do not wish to be kept alive by artificial means.

What are "artificial means"?

"Artificial means," Joe, include not only respirators, but also food and fluid—the most basic necessities of life—administered thru feeding tubes. What's so "artificial" about food and water?

And that's not the only misleading use of language, Joe. The phrase "permanently unconscious" is purely a judgmental designation fraught with error. Medical history abounds with instances of spontaneous recovery from so-called "permanently unconscious states." In many of these cases good nursing care plus the provision of food and fluid thru feeding tubes were all that was necessary for recovery. Now these would be withheld under the Living Will.

Also, Joe, the words "reasonable expectation of recovery" are much too vague. What would fulfill such a definition? When a patient's chances of recovering are 50-50, 30-70, 10-90? Even vaguer is the phrase "seriously incapacitating illness." Stroke with paralysis, diabetes, and injuries causing amputation all could be called seriously incapacitating—and this list can easily be expanded.

Another danger, Joe, is that the Living Will commands obedience from the "attending physician." The "attending physician" need not be me, your personal physician, but any physician assigned to your case in an emergency situation. His notion of a "reasonable chance of recovery" or a "seriously incapacitating illness" may not be yours or mine.

So by signing a Living Will, I might be putting my fate into the hands of a doctor I don't know and who might not have my best interest in mind?

That's right.

And there's more. The Living Will places doctors in a legal quandary. If the doctor employs "artificial" or "extraordinary" means in cases when only a minimal chance of survival exists, and the patient dies, the surviving family could make the claim that the condition was an incurable condition from the very beginning and that the doctor, therefore, violated the "Living Will." On the other hand, if the patient survives with a major disability, the patient could make a claim that the doctor inappropriately used extraordinary means in a "seriously incapacitating" illness. In marginal cases, therefore, it would become legally advantageous for the doctor not to try to save the patient at all.

Chuck Asay, by permission of the *Colorado Springs Gazette Telegraph.*

Conversely, both doctors and hospitals will feel obliged to use heroic measures on patients who have not signed "Living Wills" when these measures are not indicated, again in fear of legal action—a phenomenon similar to what we have seen in the treatment of patients who have not signed a "Do Not Resuscitate" order. This could force patients to sign Living Wills purely defensively, and would thus further entrench euthanasia.

Doc, what you're saying is that if I had signed a "Living Will" and was judged "permanently unconscious" you would be prevented from feeding me thru a feeding tube, and that I would die of starvation even though I had some chance of recovering?

Exactly, Joe!

But, Doc, before this "Living Will" business, didn't I always have the right to refuse a respirator or any other medical treatment simply by telling you?

Absolutely, Joe, and you continue to have that right without a Living Will. If you're unconscious, your family can make that decision for you. You've always had the right to refuse treatment, you have it now and you will always have it, the Living Will notwithstanding.

Then why do people sign these Living Wills?

Chiefly due to fear and confusion propagated by groups in favor of euthanasia. These groups want you to believe, Joe, that if you suffer from an incurable disease, and you're at the end of your life, breathing your last breaths, that I, your doctor, would have a breathing tube put in your trachea, against your will, put you on a respirator and keep you alive indefinitely, allowing you and your family to continue suffering. Joe, this is not true now, never was true, and never will be true. You don't need a Living Will to prevent that, you need trust in your doctor and family.

Well, Doc, it sound to me like this Living Will could be a dangerous thing, and that it really doesn't give me any options that I don't already have—so who's pushing for this Living Will and why?

Joe, the Living Will is the brainchild of the euthanasia movement. They know that if removing or withholding fluid and nutrition from patients becomes accepted and decriminalized (assisted suicide is now illegal and punishable), a major barrier to active euthanasia will have fallen. Step two will be the observation that death by starvation is a painful, drawn-out experience, and that therefore physicians should be permitted to administer lethal injections to "mercifully" end life.

Starvation Is Painful

Still, Doc, isn't it more humane to withhold food and fluid from patients who will never recover, rather than have them linger on?

Joe, death by deliberate starvation and dehydration is a very painful experience—physically painful for the patient and emotionally painful for the health care worker (usually a nurse, rarely a doctor) who has to watch it run its course. Providing patients with food and fluid is basic human care, not medical treatment, even if that nutrition is provided by way of a feeding tube. It should not be optional, just as keeping patients clean, clothed and comfortable is not optional—so far.

Food and fluid are not pharmaceuticals; they don't cure any

thing, but alleviate starvation and dehydration caused by their absence. Supplying food and water by feeding tube to a helpless, living human being is no different than feeding an equally helpless newborn by way of a baby bottle—which is just as "artificial" as a feeding tube. What those who advocate withholding feeding are really saying about people in so-called "persistent vegetative states" and other helpless, non-dying patients is that their lives are not worth the trouble or expense involved.

Favoring Death

Living Will legislation favors death as a solution to some very real and very serious human problems. Designed to *resist* treatment, Living Wills do nothing to *ensure* that a physician's hands are not tied in just those cases where his skill and modern technology may make the difference between recovery or death. A doctor caring for a patient with a Living Will may be subject to penalties (fine or imprisonment) imposed by the law if he helps a patient to live.

Julie Grimstad, *The Family*, November 1988.

Doc, how did this whole euthanasia thing get started?

Euthanasia in our time began in Germany with the publication there in 1920 of a book titled *The Release of the Destruction of Lives Devoid of Value* by Karl Bindig, a leading German jurist and Adolf Hocher, a renowned physician.

The book's concept of "lives devoid of value" or "life unworthy of life" quickly gained currency in the medical and legal professions. Soon afterwards, in 1921, 1922 and 1923, wounded German World War I veterans who obstinately refused to die were the first to be put to death by euthanasia. As the decade wore on, the practice was extended to other invalids, the handicapped and the mentally retarded.

With this groundwork accomplished by the time Hitler took power, it was a small step to justify the extermination of other groups of people deemed "burdensome" or "subhuman"—such as Jews and Gypsies—and the result was, of course, the Holocaust.

In more recent time the Netherlands has legalized euthanasia, with the result that sick elderly are fearful of entering hospitals for necessary treatment.

Do you think it could happen in our country?

Joe, euthanasia is here, now. At least 35 states already have Living Wills statutes. There has been a series of court decisions mandating the starvation and dehydration of tube-fed patients. Legislatures in states such as Hawaii are pushing to decriminalize active euthanasia by lethal injection. . . .

Already, Joe, there are politicians like ex-Governor Richard Lamm of Colorado who stated that some old people "live too long" and have a "duty to die" when their medical needs become financially burdensome.

We have Dr. Sackett of Florida who, when asked what the Living Will legislation he was advocating would accomplish, answered that it would save the State of Florida five billion dollars in ten years. In such a view, human life is nothing more than a commodity to be disposed of when it becomes too expensive to maintain.

Doc, I have the right to control my own body, so don't doctors have an obligation to do whatever I or my relatives tell them to do?

Well, Joe, now we come down to the nitty-gritty of this whole matter. Where does life come from? Who "owns life" and where does life go in the end?

The Sanctity of Life

The real answer to your question, Joe, is based on the previously secure principle that all human life has intrinsic value simply because it *is* human life, because it comes from God and is therefore sacred. We do not own it, it belongs to God and is returned to God.

"Physicians need a script on how patients want their dying and death played out."

Physicians Can Use Advance Directives to Help Dying Patients

Carl M. Kjellstrand

A 1986 survey found that while 70 percent of seriously ill patients want to discuss death and the option of limiting artificial life support measures, only 6 percent actually discuss the matter with their physicians. In the following viewpoint, Carl M. Kjellstrand argues that many physicians are reluctant to discuss these issues. He praises U.S. legislation enacted in December 1991 requiring medical institutions to discuss these subjects with their patients, arguing that the law forces both physicians and patients to confront death. Kjellstrand teaches at the University of Alberta Medical School in Edmonton, Alberta, Canada.

As you read, consider the following questions:

1. How has the medical profession mismanaged the treatment of the dying, according to Kjellstrand?
2. What does Kjellstrand conclude from the Sehgal study of patients and advance directives?
3. How can doctors improve treatment of the terminally ill, according to the author?

Carl M. Kjellstrand, "Who Should Decide About Your Death?" *Journal of the American Medical Association*, January 1, 1992, vol. 267, no. 1, pp. 104-105, © 1992, American Medical Association. Reprinted with permission.

In our technological hubris, we have mismanaged dying: the only certain ultimate outcome of all our busy efforts.

Most of us would like to die a quiet, dignified death. Anyone who works in a hospital knows that this reasonable wish is almost never fulfilled and most of us now die in hospitals. The last rites of respirators, dialysis machines, nasogastric tubes, and gastrostomy tubes along with cardiopulmonary resuscitation and the nth round of chemotherapy are wonderful when prolonging useful life but have changed death to a mechanized spectacle in which no sane person would like to be the main actor.

No One in Charge

To the patients, it often appears as if there is nobody in charge of the myriads of nurses and technicians, of attending physicians, consultants, residents, fellows, interns, administrators, and lawyers. They are right: no one is in charge. Scared physicians and cowardly hospital administrators and lawyers have abrogated their responsibility to the courts: you never get sued for doing too much. William Bartling, to be unhooked from a respirator he did not want, Peter Cinque, for relief from dialysis he hated: both had to go to court. They and Rudy Linares, who held off the intensive care unit staff at gunpoint, hugging the hopelessly ill son he had disconnected from a respirator, and the many desperate families fighting in court to stop nasogastric feeding to demented or permanently vegetative loved ones, who had said they never wanted it—all are examples of the system's inability to tame technology's torture of the dying. In an absurdity of absurdities, patients and relatives have to fight both for an entrance to and exit from the health care system. We appear to have too many high-tech scenarios that no one wants, and as more people see their aged relatives tormented and observe resuscitations depicted on television, the reaction is setting in. The medical system has been bypassed, and courts and legislatures have stepped in to try to put patients and relatives in charge of what is now often mere chaos. At least 19 states in the United States now allow relatives to order withdrawal of life support, and the Supreme Court has declared, "Yes, patients can decide." Finally, the 1991 Patient Self-Determination Act now confronts hospitals and extended care and nursing homes with the obligation to approach patients in order to find out what their wishes are in regard to life-sustaining procedures when their lives are threatened. "Good law follows good medicine" is a slogan that is here reversed. Perhaps good medicine will now follow these good laws.

We physicians have certainly not risen to the challenge. While 70% of seriously and chronically ill patients want to discuss what should be done when their life is threatened, only 6% of them have actually done so with their physician. However, the patients have not done their homework either. Less than 15% of all Americans have a living will. It is not easy to contemplate one's imminent death, although most patients feel better after a frank discussion. The law now forces all players to confront the problem.

Rob Rogers, reprinted by permission of UFS, Inc.

In [the January 1, 1992] issue of *JAMA*, Ashwini Sehgal and associates examine the consequences and uncertainties of the Patient Self-Determination Act. Their study brings the nice and lofty theories of the medical ethicists about patient self-determination into contact with the much messier reality of the real world of patient care. Sehgal's team interviewed 150 dialysis patients. The patients were chosen primarily because they were already receiving life-sustaining treatment and their choices could be presumed to be more considered and informed, but also because discontinuation of dialysis is a common cause of death in such patients. Three main questions were investigated: would the patients want dialysis discontinued should they develop Alzheimer's disease; how strictly would the patients want their advance directives followed; and third, what factors (pain, quality of life, possibility of new treatment, indignity, financial impact, and religious beliefs) should be considered by the surrogate decision maker?

The findings were that half of the patients would want dialysis discontinued if they developed Alzheimer's disease, while half would continue dialysis. Black people, more often than white, wanted dialysis to be continued. A little more than half of those interviewed (58%) decided that they would want their advance directives followed to the letter, but 42% expressed a wish to give a lot of leeway to surrogate decision makers. In multivariate analysis, only a previously executed advance directive predicted which patients wanted their wishes strictly followed. The majority of patients wanted all six factors investigated to be considered by their surrogate in making the decision. It is discouraging to note that only nine patients who had not previously discussed advance directives had taken steps to do so when contacted at follow-up, and only four of 135 had written an advance directive.

What can one conclude? The article points out uncertainties, perhaps the most important being that patients are very varied. At first glance these findings may appear to cast doubt on the effect of the law on medical practice. Why should advance directives ever be followed when there are so many different views? Of course, there will be uncertainties and individual differences in how patients react when confronted with their own imminent death. That in itself is important to know, and Sehgal and coworkers also describe how to ferret out those individual differences, so people can have a death as close as possible to the one they wish. Ask them what they want done. Ask them who should decide and with what leeway. Ask them what factors are important in the decision.

What Doctors Must Do

Where do we go from here, and how can things be improved? First, society has obviously done its part. It looked at the problem, concluded that it was bungled, and has tried to improve it by passing a law. I believe the law is a good one. It makes us confront questions from which physicians tend to shrink away but should not. What is needed from the patient is clear. Physicians need a script on how patients want their dying and death played out, and who they want the conductor to be if leeway is given. We physicians must ensure that many things are done. We need to be more open to the patient and more realistic about what we can or cannot do. We need to let patients and their relatives understand that one of the finest last acts is to let go. Students and residents need to be taught during their medical training that a complete social history must now include these sorts of questions. What would the patient want done should the ability to control events be lost? How strictly does the individual want his or her wishes followed? Who should make the final decisions? What factors are the most important for that person to consider in making such decisions? Finally, physicians need to teach themselves to recognize better the shadow line between prolonging life and prolonging dying and to understand that death should be a human act of dignity and not a prolonged mechanical failure that can be fixed with even more technology.

Physicians Do Not Need Advance Directives

Philip R. Alper

Philip R. Alper practices internal medicine in Burlingame, California. In the following viewpoint, he questions the benefits of advance directives in which patients specify in writing what kind of treatment they want in the event of terminal illness. Patients may change their minds at a later time, he writes, and may have a poor understanding of the medical alternatives available to them. Alper argues that such written legal documents are poor substitutes for a good doctor-patient relationship, in which patients discuss their wishes concerning treatment with a doctor, and the doctor respects those wishes.

As you read, consider the following questions:

1. What contrasting alternatives does Alper describe at the beginning of the viewpoint?
2. What are the limitations of living wills and advance directives, according to the author?
3. What does Alper believe is the doctor's responsibility regarding terminal care?

Philip R. Alper, "A Living Will Is a Bloodless Document," *The Wall Street Journal*, January 11, 1991. Reprinted with permission of the Wall Street Journal, © 1992, Dow Jones & Company, Inc. All Rights reserved.

"When it was Dad's time to die," my friend said, "our family doctor let us know that further measures would only prolong the agony. We cut back the intravenous fluids and medication to a symbolic trickle and he went peacefully in a few hours." I am a physician, and I remember how touched I was by the warmth and trust that helped this trio of human beings (I include the father who was comatose) make one of life's most difficult decisions.

A Strange Checklist

Contrast this with a low-cost advance directive designed and promoted by Ezekial and Linda Emanuel of Harvard Medical School. It provides a terminal-care checklist in response to four horrifying scenarios. Suppose you were in a persistent vegetative state. Or in a coma with a chance of recovery. Suppose you were demented. What if you also had a terminal illness? Just select the items you'd want—from feeding tubes to cardiac defibrillation—from the menu. Then put it in your patient file. How terribly strange.

Doctors are being told to tell patients of all the ways they may die and be kept alive—so the patients can choose. This nation has developed the notion that it is not normal to be allowed to die.

Unless a specific "Do Not Resuscitate" order is given, nursing homes in California are obliged to perform cardiopulmonary resuscitation [CPR] on 90-year-old cancer victims who do not know who or where they are. "Is he a code?" is the first thing I am likely to be asked when any older patient is admitted to the hospital, referring to Code Blue, the euphemism for CPR. Staffers worry about the need to resuscitate even when older patients are being treated for minor illnesses. They feel pressured not to do the wrong thing in the event of death—however remote the possibility.

I expect much more of this. The Supreme Court, after debating whether to remove the feeding tube from comatose Nancy Cruzan, decided to allow states to require "clear and convincing evidence" of a patient's intentions regarding terminal care, with preference for written statements. And federal law adds the requirement that all hospitals, nursing homes, HMOs and home health care-givers participating either in Medicare or Medicaid must inform every patient in writing of the right to refuse treatment and also to document whether the patient has signed an advance directive.

Complex Documents

Here in California, living wills and advance directives already have become routine in some nursing homes. The latter are three-page legalistic documents so complicated that I have trouble understanding by whom and by what authority I am being directed, let alone how I am to translate the directive into appropriate action in any one of hundreds of different clinical situations. That is, if, in an emergency, there is enough time and manpower to consult and properly evaluate the directive.

Of one thing I am certain: Patients and families trying to figure out in advance how best to handle all potential life-threatening events often say what they do not mean and vice versa.

Uncertainties of Advance Directives

There are several reasons for special doubts about whether an advance directive accurately reflects what the patient would have wanted.

Uncertainty as to how closely an advance directive reflects what a patient actually would want may arise from any of several sources. Advance directives typically require individuals to predict what they would want well in advance of the use of the directive in treatment decisionmaking, and so treatment choices in advance directives often inevitably are less well informed than competent patients' contemporaneous choices. For example, new, highly beneficial treatment may have been developed of which the patient was unaware; or if the directive is very old there may be evidence that the patient's wishes about treatment have changed. Also, advance directives must often be formulated without knowing what it will be like to experience the radically different conditions in which later treatment choices must be made. Further, advance directives are often formulated in somewhat vague or general terms, which inevitably leaves significant discretion in applying them to later treatment choices and, in turn, uncertainty about whether they have been correctly interpreted.

Dan W. Brock, *Hastings Center Report*, September/October 1991.

As a result, I never consider myself absolved of the moral responsibility of helping to reach a humane decision when continued medical efforts appear futile. This comes perilously close to ignoring the paper work that may have been executed somewhere along the line. I am a doctor, not a lawyer. I don't know whether what I see is correctly executed, whether the patient has changed his or her mind, and whether the questions have been understood the same way I do (such as the definition of "terminally ill").

Despite this raging debate, I am struck by how infrequently serious terminal-care conflicts have occurred during my nearly 30 years in practice. It is a rare person who wants to exist in a permanent vegetative state.

When an elderly patient I attended for more than a decade recently suffered a stroke followed by cardiac arrest—both entirely unexpected—the nursing staff and I instituted CPR. Within a few minutes, seeing that we failed to re-establish spontaneous breathing and an effective heartbeat, I asked the nurses, "Do you agree that we should stop?" All seemed relieved to say "yes." Later, the patient's husband of 60 years accepted my explanation that we had done all we could. I spared him the agony of making him the one to decide when and whether to stop.

The Doctor's Job

Some may consider this playing God. But I acted on the basis of my knowledge of the people and the way in which they looked to me for medical care. After 10 years with a patient, giving up isn't easy. But it is the doctor's job to know when to try and when to quit. I tell this to patients who ask me about terminal care. Never have they rejected my offer to treat them as I would like to be treated myself. I file the living wills but state my belief that mutual trust is what matters most.

Nor have families of patients unable to speak for themselves often caused the kind of problems that make for good TV scripts—the relative who can't wait to get his hands on the money or the one who refuses to ever allow the patient to die because of some ulterior motive or guilt. I make sure that the staff, the family and I reach a meeting of the minds that reaffirms our common humanity and loyalty to the ill or injured patient. This may result in reducing the intravenous fluids and medications to a symbolic trickle rather than brutally "pulling the plug."

I am strengthened by the thought that my patients have *chosen* me as their personal physician. They particularly want me to be around when they are receiving highly specialized care from physicians who barely know them. It is here where there is more reason for concern that allegiance to technology, fear of lawsuits and simple inertia could turn any one of us into a Nancy Cruzan.

No living will or advance directive entirely takes the place of dealing with a doctor you know and trust. Stories are already making the medical rounds about the wife who, based on her husband's advance directive, refused permission to put him on a respirator. In her agitation, she didn't see the difference between temporary and permanent respirator therapy. Fortunately, the attending physician overruled her protest, used the respirator and delivered a healthy husband back to her.

Making Terminal Treatment Decisions

Deciding how to treat terminally ill people has become a complex question in this medically advanced age. Many people now worry about being kept alive by artificial means long past the point of what they consider to be a meaningful life. Other people do not have these concerns and would prefer to have their lives prolonged as long as possible. These views may change with time or circumstances. For example, some terminally ill patients may wish to continue treatment as long as their pain can be controlled but may change their minds about treatment if their pain becomes overwhelming.

In this exercise you will be asked to make some decisions regarding your own terminal care by filling out a sample advance medical directive. Then you will be asked to discuss your decisions.

Part I

The following is adapted and simplified from a medical directive created by Linda L. Emanuel and Ezekiel J. Emanuel, two Boston-based physicians. It describes three situations and gives you choices of various medical treatments. Working by yourself, read the directive, decide which treatments you would agree to, and check the appropriate boxes.

Situation (A)

You are in a persistent vegetative state and, in the opinion of your physician and several consultants, have only a small chance of regaining consciousness and virtually no hope of recovering your reasoning powers. Your body can be kept alive indefinitely. What would be your wishes concerning the following treatments, should your doctors determine that you need them?

Situation (B)

You have a brain disease that makes you unable to recognize people or speak understandably. You also have a terminal illness that will likely cause your death. What would be your wishes concerning the following treatments, should your doctors determine that you need them?

Situation (C)

You have brain damage which makes you unable to recognize people or to communicate, but you have no terminal illness and may live in this condition for a long time. What would be your wishes concerning the following treatments, should your doctors determine that you need them?

Treatment One: Mechanical breathing. Breathing maintained by a respirator or other machine. Can be used temporarily to clear up infections or permanently if patient cannot breathe on his own.

Treatment Two: Artificial nutrition and hydration. Nutrition and fluids given through a tube in the nose, veins, or stomach. Used in cases where patient cannot be fed through the mouth. If withdrawn, patient dies for lack of food and water.

Treatment Three: Chemotherapy. Drugs used to fight cancer. They often cause side effects, including hair loss, nausea, and vomiting.

Treatment Four: Pain medication. May dull consciousness and hasten the moment of death.

	Situation (A)				Situation (B)				Situation (C)			
Treatment	Yes	No	Undecided	Trial*	Yes	No	Undecided	Trial	Yes	No	Undecided	Trial
One												
Two												
Three												
Four												

*Trial: indicates that you wish the physicians to attempt the treatment, but discontinue if it is ineffective.

Part II

The whole class should discuss the following questions.

1. Do you think your feelings on treatment might change in the future? Would you feel comfortable making your decision legally binding?

2. How comfortable would you feel with your family making such decisions in lieu of any written directives from you?

3. Do you believe economic concerns, such as the cost of continued medical treatment and hospitalization, should play any role in making such decisions?

Periodical Bibliography

The following articles have been selected to supplement the diverse views presented in this chapter.

George J. Annas	"The Health Care Proxy and the Living Will," *The New England Journal of Medicine*, April 25, 1991. Available from 10 Shattuck St., Boston, MA 02115-6094.
Allan S. Brett	"Limitations of Listing Specific Medical Interventions in Advance Directives," *Journal of the American Medical Association*, August 14, 1991. Available from the American Medical Association, 515 N. State St., Chicago, IL 60610.
Dan W. Brock	"Trumping Advance Directives," in "Practicing the PSDA," Special Supplement, *Hastings Center Report*, September/October 1991.
B.D. Colen	"The Woman Who Wouldn't Die," *Redbook*, March 1989.
Richard Doerflinger	"Right to Life or Right to Die?" *The Family*, January 1992. Available from the Daughters of St. Paul, 50 St. Paul's Avenue, Boston, MA 02130.
Linda L. and Ezekiel J. Emanuel	"The Medical Directive," *Journal of the American Medical Association*, June 9, 1989.
Deborah M. House	"Advance Medical Directives and the Role of the Church," *The Christian Century*, December 4, 1991.
David Orentlicher	"Advance Medical Directives," *Journal of the American Medical Association*, May 2, 1990.
Kenneth R. Overberg	"Preparing Now for the Hour of Death," *St. Anthony Messenger*, April 1991.
Doug Podolsky	"A Right-to-Die Reminder," *U.S. News & World Report*, December 2, 1991.
John Poppy	"End Game," *Esquire*, August 1990.
Andrew Purvis	"When the Patient Calls the Shots," *Time*, December 9, 1991.
Ashwini Sehgal et al.	"How Strictly Do Dialysis Patients Want Their Advance Directives Followed?" *Journal of the American Medical Association*, January 1, 1992.
Susan M. Wolf et al.	"Sources of Concern About the Patient Self-Determination Act," *The New England Journal of Medicine*, December 5, 1991.

How Should One Cope with Grief?

DEATH AND DYING

Chapter Preface

Most people, in addition to having to confront the reality of their own death, must at some point in their lives cope with the death of a spouse, parent, relative, friend, or child. The death of a loved one is usually traumatic and can often have long-lasting repercussions. The emotions an individual experiences after a death are part of the grieving process.

This process has been extensively studied by psychiatrists. Some have identified different stages people pass through, including denial, anger, and acceptance. Whether all people from all societies pass through similar stages is a matter of debate. In the following chapter, a variety of viewpoints consider the process of grieving and how individuals and society help or hinder that process.

"Grief . . . is a process, one that moves from denial and avoidance to recognition and acceptance of loss. "

Grief Follows a Predictable Pattern

Patricia Anderson

Psychologists and doctors have developed several theories on the grieving process, most of which identify stages or steps most mourners go through. In the following viewpoint, Patricia Anderson describes four stages of grief: initial shock, searching, despair, and acceptance. She describes how most grievers move through this process, and how those who do not often develop psychological problems. Anderson is a writer and television producer whose books include *Affairs in Order: A Complete Resource Guide to Death and Dying*, from which this viewpoint is taken.

As you read, consider the following questions:

1. Why is it important to acknowledge grief, according to Anderson?
2. According to the author, what are some of the symptoms of pathological grief?
3. What resources can a person turn to for help in the grieving process, according to Anderson?

The absolute finality of death creates a kind of loss that is unlike any other. This loss can be the most profound experience of life and also the most painful. Grief, as the expression of that pain, is part of a healing process enabling us to survive loss and to continue to function in the world.

A Personal Response

Grief is essentially a private experience. How each of us responds to the death of someone we love is uniquely our own, personal response. However, the way in which we express that private feeling is influenced by what is acceptable in the larger society. Mourning ceremonies (funeral and memorial services) are models for the culturally accepted form of grieving, setting the tone and defining the manner of our expression.

Different societies have radically different approaches: In some cultures in the East, survivors are expected to sob and wail openly, exhibiting their sadness and dismay, while in Japan the bereaved family smiles so as not to burden others. What is considered an appropriate public display in one society is frowned on in another.

Time also influences custom. In Victorian England, death was romanticized and mourning was an elaborate ritual entailing black wreaths, bunting hung on doorways, and "mourning dress" worn for years after the event.

In this country today, however, we have decreased the number and nature of public symbols of mourning and discourage a prolonged expression of grief. We expect feelings to be controlled and mourning to be brief. Open demonstrations of intense grief embarrass us. Survivors are often encouraged to keep a stiff upper lip and disguise their deepest emotions with a display of false reserve. This can cause problems. . . .

When the funeral or memorial service is over, grief is often just beginning. The disorienting feelings that arise in bereavement can become quite intense and last a long time. If unexpressed and unresolved, they can lead to serious emotional difficulties resulting in, for instance, self-destructive behavior or an impaired ability to function. Thus, it is important to acknowledge bereavement, to experience and resolve grief, and eventually to find a way through the pain.

The Grief Process

Psychologists and psychiatrists have developed a number of theories about how grief works. Although they differ in some respects, many of these theories share common elements, identifying stages or phases of the grief process and agreeing generally about the nature of reactions over time.

Grief is not a static condition, constant and unchanging. It is a process, one that moves from denial and avoidance to recognition and acceptance of loss.

Keeping in mind how widely responses will vary from one person to another, the grief process generally includes the following stages:

- Initial shock and denial
- Yearning or searching for the lost person
- Disorientation and despair
- Adapting, acceptance, and recovery

Initial shock The first reaction to death, especially sudden death, tends to be shock, numbness, and often, denial. It is the psychological equivalent of the kind of physiological reaction we experience when we suffer a serious physical trauma—our body goes into shock, slowing down all nonessential functions until basic equilibrium can be regained.

Stages of Grief

One way to think about the grieving process is to consider its four normally accepted stages: shock and denial; guilt, anger, and withdrawal; depression; and resolution.

Grieving is a process which the bereaved person travels through to reach the next phase of adjustment. The stages are connected and people can go back and forth between them (sometimes within the period of a few minutes). Members of the same family may be in various phases and move at different rates.

Catherine Thompson and Barbara E. Moore, *USA Today*, July 1991.

Emotional shock and numbness allow us to delay the realization of death until we are capable of taking it in. The magnitude of loss inflicted by the death of someone we love is often so great that we cannot comprehend it all at once. Because immediate realization of the totality of the loss would overwhelm us, shock permits the masking of truth, at least in part. It allows us to recognize just a small piece of the truth at a time.

Bodily Symptoms

All of the physiological symptoms of shock, fear, and anxiety may show themselves during this initial period. A racing heart, dizziness or even faintness, appetite loss or stomach trouble, restlessness and insomnia, are all common symptoms of this reaction.

Physical shock and psychological denial are also a way of protesting against reality. Denial is our way to try to discredit the information, to cancel the news, to keep it away.

Searching As the initial shock subsides and the survivor begins to grasp reality, many psychologists have remarked that survivors seek to retrieve or locate the dead person. This searching phase may involve calling out to the deceased, even expecting a response. The bereaved may become preoccupied with thoughts of the loved one or repeatedly recall painful memories. Persistently hoping for the return of the deceased is a common feature of this searching phase.

We search not only for the one who has died but for our role in their absence. During this time, a grieving person may move as if on remote control, retaining the numbness of the initial shock. In the wake of death, survivors frequently feel lost themselves, "abandoned" by the deceased, and confused, insecure, fearful, and alone.

Disorientation and despair As the bereaved begins to accept the fact that the deceased is never coming back, the pain of the loss can really hit hard. Increasing awareness can bring the release of any number of very powerful emotions—anguish, despair, depression, hopelessness, anger, guilt. In many cases, the most powerful and prominent emotions will be anger and guilt. This is a normal reaction.

Anger

Feeling that something horrible has happened, we may seek someone to blame. Anger can be directed at anyone—a police officer who informed you of the death, doctors, nurses, family members, or friends. Or it may be directed toward the deceased; you may feel s/he has abandoned you.

But in all likelihood you will serve as the primary target of your own anger. Many people find it much easier to be angry at themselves than at others. In confronting the death of someone they loved, survivors sometimes reproach themselves for their failings in the relationship. You might have thoughts such as "I should have" done this, or "if only" I'd done that s/he would still be alive. This kind of second-guessing guilt can become especially severe in circumstances such as accidental death or suicide. Guilt and self-blame are common reactions and can be the most difficult aspects of grief to overcome.

Adapting, acceptance, and recovery Acceptance of loss comes slowly and inconsistently rather than all at once. The bereaved may feel better for a while and then very much worse. In 1990, the *Harvard Medical School Mental Health Letter* ran a series of articles on bereavement in which the editors state:

> It takes time to accept the reality of the loss emotionally as well as intellectually. Depression and emotional swings may last as long as several years. A kind of recovery is achieved when the bereaved can finally think of the dead person without overwhelming sadness and invest energy in other thoughts

and activities. As the new reality is acknowledged and assimilated, grief fades into treasured memories.

Adapting to a death and being able to function in the world, eventually forming new bonds, is the goal of the grief process. However, as the above article points out, "A new identity and social role are achieved, but recovery is never complete. Some effects last a lifetime, and waves of grief may return for many years on birthdays or the anniversary of the death."

These phases, as defined by mental health professionals, are loose guidelines for discussing the nature of grief. Such a model may or may not describe your particular experience, but most people do find a way through the difficult early disorientation to some form of acceptance or adaptation.

The way each of us responds to death depends on many factors, including age, gender, maturity, intelligence, cultural conditioning, and ethnic or religious influences. The manner in which someone dies also has a significant impact on the way in which survivors experience grief. Psychologists call this "the death surround." Factors here include the location, the reason and type of death, and the degree of preparation. Sudden or accidental death and suicide generally involve more bereavement complications than a death that had been long expected. . . .

Good Grief

When psychologists talk about "resolving grief as a goal of the bereavement process," they are speaking of reaching a point where loss has been acknowledged and accepted and the survivor is able to function in the world. This isn't easy if you've lost someone you love.

Initially, you may have trouble getting through the day—or the night. Simply coping with the practical requirements of life may be a tremendous challenge. But eventually, if grief takes its course, you will be able to think of the deceased without crying or suffering unduly, to express regrets without feeling guilt, and to love others without a fear that you are betraying the deceased.

For many bereaved people, being able to remember the deceased without falling apart provides the first big sign that they are beginning to move through the process. Other signs include being able to forget the deceased for a while without feeling guilty, being able to enjoy yourself without feeling guilty, looking forward to the future, and seeing the death in perspective. In the case of the death of a spouse or partner, forming new friendships signals a turning point in recovery. Although this goal may seem impossible or even undesirable when you first begin to grieve, new friendships do signal a willingness to resume life without the deceased.

Successfully working through grief doesn't mean that you forget the deceased or that you stop missing him or her. It does mean that you can live your life in spite of your loss.

Bad Grief

In some cases, the progress of grief goes awry along the way. Symptoms of problems can take any of the following forms: a pronounced absence or inhibition of grief, prolonged or excessive grief, or the distortion of grief. These "atypical" behaviors prevent the bereaved from entering into a new life.

Psychiatrist Colin Parkes points out that these atypical forms do not really differ from normal grief in any of its symptoms or reactions but simply in the intensity and duration of the reactions. It's as if the mourner got stuck in one of the usual phases of grief (shock, anger, or guilt for instance), distorting, intensifying, or prolonging a typical reaction and making it chronic.

A Healing Process

In normal circumstances, grief is a psychophysiologic process that leads to the gradual acceptance of the loss of the loved one and to a renewed capacity to invest emotional energy in other people and new life activities. The outcome of the process varies considerably with the age, personality, strengths, and life situation of the bereaved person. Various stages of grieving have been described, beginning with psychological shock or numbing and preoccupation with the lost person. These are usually followed by a state similar to depression, with such psychological and physiologic reactions as sadness, withdrawal, anhedonia, loss of energy, and insomnia. However, normal grief is not generally associated with the morbid sense of worthlessness or prolonged functional impairment common in clinical depression.

Malcolm P. Rogers and Peter Reich, *The New England Journal of Medicine*, August 25, 1988.

Absence of Grief An apparent absence of the symptoms of grief does not usually indicate that the mourner doesn't feel the loss, only that s/he has delayed any reaction. Although sometimes due to the prolongation of the shock or denial reaction, absence of grief can be an act of will. The apparent lack—which prohibits resolution—may yield to either prolonged or distorted forms of mourning.

Psychologists point out that people may actively prevent themselves from grieving for any number of reasons. They may have a pronounced fear of losing control of themselves or their grief. This anxiety often stems from cultural conditioning that depicts the uncontrolled expression of emotion as "weak." Bereaved people might also stop themselves from grieving for fear that reviewing the relationship would unearth guilt or anger—feelings regarded as unacceptable toward a dead loved one. Finally, if the relationship was not recognized by the larger society, the bereaved might not feel "allowed" to mourn over it.

Excessive Grief Excessive grief involves an unconscious unwillingness to let the deceased go. Months and even years can elapse following the death of a loved one, but excessive grievers may still maintain the characteristics of a recent bereavement. They may refuse to form new relationships. Chronic mourners cling to the deceased, almost as if they were keeping the dead alive through their prolonged grief. Some may fear that to overcome the loss would somehow betray a tacit pact with the deceased never to live a life separate from him or her. They cling to the pain of loss because it is all they have left of the loved one.

Certain types of death seem to demand protracted periods of grief in order to adapt to the loss. The death of a child, for instance, generally requires a longer period of bereavement than the death of an aged parent. Similarly, it usually takes longer to move toward acceptance of a sudden and unexpected death—especially a suicide—than it does to grieve over a death that follows an extended terminal illness. However, if symptoms appropriate in acute grief persist too long without changing, it can be a sign that the survivor needs professional help in coming to terms with the loss.

Distorted Grief Distorted grief manifests itself primarily through self-destructive acts, obsessive thoughts of self-destruction, or extreme mental or emotional aberrations. Prolonged inattention to basic survival needs, such as eating and sleeping, or social needs, such as friendships and social activities, are symptomatic of distorted grief.

How to Find Help

In 1917, Sigmund Freud wrote,

> It is well worth notice that, although mourning involves grave departures from the normal attitude to life, it never occurs to us to regard it as a pathological condition and to refer it to medical treatment. We rely on its being overcome after a certain lapse of time, and we look upon any interference with it as useless or even harmful.

While it is true that grief is a normal response to loss, it may be that today it is more difficult to cope with that response on our own. Often we do not have the support of a large, extended family or of ritualized customs that maintain us throughout a lengthy mourning period. And while the psychopathic condition of necrophobia (an abnormal fear of death) would not be ascribed to most "normal" people, we do, as a society, suffer from a cultural or mass necrophobia. It adversely affects us all by creating a general environment in which a positive death experience is very difficult to achieve and grief is an embarrassment. If we never allow ourselves to think about death, we don't know how to deal with bereavement. Most people need support during mourning, often beyond that available from family and friends. Psychotherapy, counseling, or other professional help can provide that support.

Bereavement counseling is becoming more specialized as mental health professionals develop a better understanding of how to assist with the grief process. In looking for a good clinician, you should try to find one of these specialists, someone who works specifically with grief and who has experience with the type of bereavement you are dealing with (anticipated, sudden, or violent death, suicide, etc.).

Another resource is a self-help support group. Filling the void left by the vanishing extended family, peer support groups have developed to address many specialized needs, from widows and widowers to families of suicide victims. Since members of these groups have gone through similar experiences, they can often provide advice or support in a more informed manner than could a relative or friend. Chances are a self-help group exists nearby that can help you deal with the particular circumstances of your bereavement.

"The truth is that there is no universal prescription for how to grieve."

Grief May Not Follow a Predictable Pattern

Daniel Goleman

Many psychologists and bereavement counselors argue that people who grieve go through several predictable patterns, and recommend counseling for those who fail to follow these patterns. In the following viewpoint, Daniel Goleman examines several scientific studies that dispute these theories. People grieve in a variety of ways, Goleman writes. Some people show little sign of distress, while others remain troubled for a long time. Such reactions should not be considered abnormal, he concludes. Goleman, a former senior editor for *Psychology Today*, writes for the *New York Times*.

As you read, consider the following questions:

1. How do the surveys on grief examined by Goleman differ from previous scientific studies on the subject?
2. According to the author, what are some grieving behaviors that psychotherapists have mistakenly labeled as abnormal?
3. How do the circumstances of death alter the grieving process, according to the author?

Some of the most widespread beliefs about mourning are largely myths, new scientific findings are showing. And researchers warn that these myths can increase the mourners' distress by holding them to false expectations of what is "normal."

The new studies have monitored the course of grief more closely than ever before. Compared with what had been supposed, they show a far wider range of normal reactions to a grave loss—the death of a loved one, say, or the paralysis that follows spinal injury.

More Myth than Fact

Elements of the prevailing wisdom that now seem more myth than fact include the idea that "healthy" grieving includes a period of intense distress or depression shortly after the loss, that failure to have such feelings bodes poorly for psychological adjustment and that the mourner should get over the loss after a finite period of grieving.

The new findings suggest that psychotherapists are too quick to see pathology in other reactions that are actually normal. "I don't say there is no such thing as pathology in mourning," said Camille Wortman, a psychologist at the University of Michigan, who did much of the new research. "But the data show we need to expand our notions of what is a normal reaction to loss."

Five different studies of widows and widowers, she said, have found that between a quarter and two-thirds of those who are grieving are not greatly distressed. On the other hand, a study showed that people who lost a child or spouse in an auto accident were likely to be depressed and anxious years later.

"Because of their expectations, people are prone to being too judgmental of someone who, say, does not seem to be distressed enough immediately after a loss or who stays upset for what seems to others to be too long," Dr. Wortman said.

Although there is a large body of clinical wisdom about grief, Dr. Wortman said it is largely based on studies of people who have sought therapy for their problems. Until the last five years or so, there have been few carefully designed studies that systematically tracked for several years the emotional course of ordinary people who have suffered a grave loss.

The study of the parents and spouses of auto accident victims was typical of the new approach. Dr. Wortman and her colleagues sought out 80 such survivors four or more years after the fatal accident. Researchers went to their homes and interviewed each for two and a half hours about the impact of the death on their life and about their emotional and psychological state.

Even four to seven years after the loss, many still had painful thoughts and felt distressed. Many of those who lost children said they still could not put the deaths out of their minds, and often dwelled on the specifics of the fatal accidents. They were more depressed, hostile and worried in general than a comparable group who had not had such losses.

A Range of Reactions

A . . . study done by the Institute of Medicine (IOM) of the National Academy of Sciences concludes that bereavement is associated with measurable distress in everyone, but that the distress can range greatly in intensity and duration. A survivor's way of life commonly is disturbed for at least one year but may be affected for as long as three years. And there is tremendous variation in the way people react to bereavement. These reactions, the report says, cannot be neatly plotted in a series of well-defined stages, nor is the progression from the time of death to the resolution of bereavement likely to be in a straight line. There are a number of psychological, social and biological processes that interact and make it difficult to define a normal reaction to bereavement.

Christopher Joyce, *Psychology Today*, November 1984.

In an article in the July 1989 issue of the *Journal of Clinical and Consulting Psychology*, Dr. Wortman and Roxane Cohen Silver, a psychologist at the University of California at Los Angeles, review this and other research findings that strongly challenge several beliefs about the emotional course of coming to grips with a devastating loss.

Distress Not Inevitable

For example, Dr. Wortman says it is not inevitable that severe distress or depression must follow a loss. Nor is the absence of such a response necessarily "pathological."

These assumptions, made part of the canon of psychotherapy by giants like Freud and the British psychoanalyst John Bowlby, were repeated in 1984 in an influential report on bereavement by the Institute of Medicine, a part of the National Academy of Science. But Dr. Wortman reviews new data rebutting the assumption that everyone who is mentally healthy will undergo such a period of distress.

The new studies used systematic criteria for evaluating distress, including assessments by friends and relatives of the mourner. They found that a sizable minority do not seem to go through such a period of distress. For instance, a 1986 study of Mormons who had recently lost a spouse showed that only about one in five were seriously depressed in the months that followed.

Friends or family members may find such people cold and unloving; therapists may think they are denying their own feelings. But Dr. Wortman argues that many or most may be exhibiting a psychological strength that allows them to go through mourning relatively unshaken. To be sure, they are sad; they cry and miss the loved one. But they do not exhibit intense distress, they manage to carry on their lives with little difficulty and they never become deeply depressed.

Grief Is Borne Lightly

"People don't realize how common it is for grief to be borne lightly," Dr. Wortman said. "Nor is there any compelling evidence that they are denying the loss or did not truly love the person. If they were denying the loss, they would go out of their way to avoid thoughts of the loved one, but we don't find that to be the case. Nor are they unloving in recalling the relationship: there's no evidence it was full of conflict in any way, or that they weren't really attached to the person."

The absence of extreme distress "can be a sign of resilience," she said, "but that possibility has never been considered."

One trait common among such people is a set of beliefs that give them a broader perspective. Dr. Wortman said, "Many of them have world views—often a spiritual outlook—that lets them see the loss in a way they can accept: part of life's plan, for example, or for some greater purpose."

Dr. Wortman grants that the failure to be greatly distressed can be a result of emotional numbness or an unhealthy denial of the reality of the loss, both of which can later give way to a flood of distress. But she said the data she has collected show that if people are not greatly distressed at first after a loss, they probably never will be.

And those who are most upset immediately after a loss tend to be among the most upset a year or two later. The findings call into question the widespread assumption that a period of severe distress leads to a more balanced adjustment.

The new data lead Dr. Wortman to conclude that people who are the most upset by a loss are at greatest risk for emotional difficulties in the long run. And contrary to clinical lore that lack of distress just after the loss leads to "delayed grief," those who have a relatively mild initial reaction seem to stay less distressed.

Periods of Mourning

Another belief challenged by the new data is that mourners should have recovered from the loss within some set period, reaching a final stage of recovery or acceptance. "Failure to reach this stage is seen as a sign of 'pathological' mourning in virtually every major work on the subject," Dr. Wortman said.

"But the data say otherwise." Such people may benefit from therapy to help them deal with their depression and anxiety, but this does not mean they are abnormal.

Grieving May Last Years

The feelings of grief last far longer than society in general allows. Even closest friends may expect us to be back to "normal" in a few weeks after a death. But living with loss is not so simple. The death of someone close may cause emotional pain and confusion for months or even years. Losing someone we love through death is one of the most traumatic of life's experiences. Acute grief affects several million people every year.

Nancy O'Connor, *Letting Go With Love*, 1984.

A 1983 Harvard study of widows and widowers found that 40 percent were still anxious and depressed as long as four years after the death of their spouse.

"It was a surprise to find that so many people still felt distress that many years after a loss," said Robert Weiss, a social psychologist now with the Work and Family Research Unit at the University of Massachusetts at Boston, who did the study while at Harvard.

Dr. Weiss, who did his research with Colin Parkes, a psychiatrist at London University Hospital, added: "Before we started publishing our results, the general expectation among the public and psychotherapists alike was that there would normally be deep grief up to the time of the funeral, and then a continuing sadness for a few months and withdrawal from fully active social life for a year. Psychological recovery was expected within three or four months."

Dr. Weiss and other researchers are concluding that apart from the differences between mourners, the kind of death can make a great deal of difference. Untimely or sudden deaths are generally harder to get over. And the death of a child can be the hardest of all.

"Perhaps the worst kind of death to mourn is the sudden loss of a child to a drunk driver," said Dr. Wortman. "It's unexpected, untimely and caused by someone else's negligence. You lose not just a loved one, but your basic beliefs about how just the world is."

The Search for Meaning

Psychotherapists have long considered it a necessary end to the grieving process that people finally find some sort of meaning in the loss that allows them to make peace with it.

But in the Harvard study of those who were widowed, and in a study by Dr. Wortman of parents whose infants died suddenly, up to four years later about 40 percent of those who mourned were still asking why the loss had occurred. More than half who had lost a loved one in an auto accident failed to find any "meaning" in it four to seven years later.

The new findings do not change what psychotherapists see as the need to help some people with mourning. "The fact that many people have a given pattern, such as emotional numbness after the death, or great distress years later, still means you can do something to help them do better with their feelings about the loss," said Bram Fridhandler, a psychologist at the University of California at San Francisco. Dr. Fridhandler is one of several researchers conducting a study of people having troubles with grief.

"The determination of whether grief is pathological or not goes way beyond whether there seems to be too little or too much distress," said Dr. Fridhandler. "You need to consider how much it disrupts people's other relationships, or ability to work, or the extent to which they dwell on a death when they try to think of something else."

Researchers hope the new results will make others more understanding of those who are grieving but who do not fit preconceived notions of how they should feel or act.

"People who are grieving often find themselves under a subtle social pressure to show more distress than they may feel close to the loss, on the one hand, and to cheer up and get on with life long before they feel able to do so, on the other," said Dr. Wortman. "The truth is that there is no universal prescription for how to grieve, and that we are just beginning to realize the full range of normal grief."

"Let your heart break. Let go of the suffering
that keeps you back from life."

Cope with Death by Openly Grieving

Stephen Levine

Stephen Levine has for several years counseled the terminally
ill. He has worked with Elisabeth Kübler-Ross and for seven
years directed the Hanumna Dying Project. A consultant to a
number of hospice, hospital, and mediation groups, he is the co-
author of *A Gradual Awakening* and *Who Dies?* The following
viewpoint is excerpted from his book *Meetings at the Edge*,
which consists of a series of dialogues between his patients and
himself. In this selection, the author describes a woman,
Dorothy, who is having a difficult time dealing with her young
daughter's impending death. Levine suggests she openly grieve
for her daughter, which in turn helps resolve both her daughter's fear and her own reluctance to accept death.

As you read, consider the following questions:

1. Why does the author discourage Dorothy from hiding her
   feelings from her daughter?
2. What suggestions does Levine give to Dorothy?
3. How does the grieving process bring Dorothy closer to her
   daughter, according to the author?

From *Meetings at the Edge* by Stephen Levine. Copyright © 1984 by Stephen Levine.
Reprinted by permission of Doubleday, a division of Bantam Doubleday Dell Publishing
Group.

Dorothy called one morning to say that her nine-year-old daughter was dying of lymphoma. After an unexpected, six-week illness the lymph nodes had begun "popping up like popcorn," to which she added, "It feels to me and to the doctors as if it is already a bit too late for any sort of intervention."

S: "Does you daughter understand what is happening to her?"

D: "No, not entirely. She asked me the other day, 'Mom, I am really pretty sick, aren't I?' and I said, 'Little girls nine years old don't usually get so lumpy.'"

Her mother added, "We will take it quiet now and do the things we are able to do. She has been out of school but I have not pressed it. She asked me what they were running the test for and I said cancer. And she said, 'People die with that, don't they?' And I said, 'Certainly they die with that and they also die crossing the streets.' I tried to be very casual with her."

I asked Dorothy if she thought her fear at that moment may have caused her to miss a moment of truth. If indeed her daughter wasn't trying to see past the barrier of Dorothy's motherhood and protection to some place essential where she could share her fears and her confusion of what she was moving toward.

D: "At this point, as long as she is active, I am not going to say much of what is happening. The night before last two lymph nodes in her groin began swelling and one on her neck about three days before that. And she said, 'Why am I getting these, Mom?'"

I mentioned to Dorothy that she sounded very matter-of-fact. That rather than holding back, as painful as it might be, perhaps she might investigate more deeply what she felt, and I asked her, "What if your daughter died tonight? What would remain unsaid? What have you not shared with her that you might wish to?" To which she replied, "At first I cried at night, but in the days I try to deal with it objectively." I pointed out that her daughter only saw her during the day, however; that her daughter might benefit from sharing in some of those tears so she might see some of the softness that her mother felt at night when they were both apart. Dorothy said, "I decided not to go through all that."

Deciding on Feeling

S: "Do you think emotions are something you can just decide about?"

D: "To a large extent, yes, at least the display of them."

S: "What seems inappropriate about sharing your concern?"

D: "At this point I would just like to try and remain as normal as humanly possible."

S: "What do you mean by normal? Isn't the sharing of this

146

grief normal under the circumstances? Mightn't it open a deeper contact between you two, a healing of the confusion and isolation which is frightening to you both? Truly, you can't go through the door with her, but you can accompany her more fully to the threshold."

Experience the Pain of Grief

Part of coming to grips with the reality of death is experiencing the emotional and physical pain caused by the loss. Many people in the denial stage of grieving attempt to avoid pain by choosing to reject the emotions and feelings they are experiencing. Some do this by avoiding places and circumstances that remind them of the deceased. I know of one widow who quit playing golf and stopped eating at a particular restaurant because these were activities that she had enjoyed with her husband. Another widow found it extremely painful to be with her dead husband's twin, even though he and her sister-in-law were her most supportive friends. . . .

The problem with the avoidance strategy is that it is impossible to escape the pain associated with mourning. According to John Bowlby, "Sooner or later, some of those who avoid all conscious grieving, break down—usually with some form of depression." Tears can afford cleansing for wounds created by loss, and fully experiencing the pain ultimately provides wonderful relief to those who suffer, while eliminating long-term chronic grief.

Michael Leming, *Understanding Death, Dying, and Bereavement*, 1990.

D: "I have felt so alone for the past weeks and I guess she must too. I have lost so much in life. My husband died of cancer three years ago. I have lost two other children to cancer as well. There is so much grief, I don't know where to start. I think basically we are always alone. I don't like it but I don't know what to do about it."

S: "You have pushed so much away that now it seems impossible to make room for it all, but that is your daughter's legacy to you. Each grief demands to be recognized—the pain around your heart is its voice. Can you feel that sensation in the middle of your chest over your heart?"

D: "No."

S: "No soreness?"

D: "Well, yes."

I explored with Dorothy that she might find a quiet place in the house some evening and start to focus on that sensation in the center of her chest. To start to open to whatever pain arose there because the heart armors itself, and her work now is to allow her heart to be torn open to the truths of the present moment. Focusing on the sensation, she might find that it would become very distinct and that she could start breathing directly into it as though it were a vent opening into her heart. That the soreness was the touch point of her heart, and as she entered this great soreness of heart all sorts of associated images might arise in the mind, glimpses of the deaths of others and the hard swallowing of long-held tears. To open to this fear and notice how it forms a shell around each stiff breath. To meet this fear with a willingness to be in this pain as a means of going beyond it into the vast love just beneath. If she wished her heart to touch her daughter's heart, she must focus on whatever old grief and broken longings blocked that touch point. I shared with her that this was not a time to seek safe territory as obviously there was no way she could protect her daughter from the experience of this time. All she could do was open in love to these precious moments that remained.

S: "How merciless we are with ourselves. How little we are available to ourselves and to others when we are maintaining this sort of self-protection which we have been told to cultivate our whole life through. Indeed, your daughter's teaching for you may be to start to tune in to the suffering which has so long been present in your heart. But by pulling back, as you have so many times in the past, you may find just another dark veil drawn across the heart, another moment missed that you wish to share with your daughter. I know it is a tough one."

Childhood Memories of Death

Dorothy shared with me her fear of opening to those feelings. "When I was a child, I was given a puppy for Christmas, a little cocker spaniel. He was like one of my dolls—but better—he was alive—but he got run over two months later and that same week my grandmother died—no one wanted to hear about my puppy and we weren't allowed to talk about Grandma. I guess I just didn't know what to do with it all—something in me shut down, I guess. I've put each death in my life behind me as quickly as possible. I almost never cry. I would like to get out all this grief but it sounds like such a bummer."

S: "How much more of a bummer is it to feel cut off from the world? From your daughter at a time of such need? We keep guarding our heart—we want to be so together, and in being so together we retract from the world into a kind of drowsy blindness that lets life slip by unshared."

D: "But it has always seemed so much safer to hold back from all this pain."

S: "That is what we have so often been encouraged to do. But you know, it is pretty hard to kiss someone who is keeping a stiff upper lip. How does this stiffness feel? Does it leave you sore all over? Where is the safety? You can't keep from dying, you can't keep your heart from aching—the pain just becomes more unbearable, seemingly unworkable. You have to do exactly what you wish your daughter to do right now—to open, to soften around the pain, to make contact with something essential. All the holding back of a lifetime has become focused now in this predicament. It is time to be kind to yourself, to use these days or weeks as a deepening of your opening to life—by just loving her and being with her as your heart allows.

Death Is Not the Enemy

"As we speak now, just close your eyes and gently move into the pain. Allow the heart's armoring to melt. There is a vastness you share with your daughter. An edgeless unity with her, and all that is, which can be discovered when the heart allows itself to be torn open. Allow the pain to penetrate into the very center of your heart. Let go of any resistance that falsely assures you it is your only defense. Share in the deathlessness of just being in the moment, with whatever it offers. Allowing yourself to go beyond the defenses of the mind. Move into the very heart of the moment. It can allow an experience of much greater context than the fearful attachment to the body. This is the unfinished work we are so frightened to move into. Clearly death is not the enemy. It is our lack of self-trust. Our forgetfulness of the extraordinary nature which inhabits this tiny body for a moment. I don't mean just your daughter's tiny body. I mean your tiny body as well. Go gently through without force. Just opening a moment at a time to the feelings and pain that arise there in the middle of your chest. With great kindness to yourself, remember how force, again and again, closes the heart."

D: "You know, even though my mind is fighting against what you are saying, the sensation in my heart is beginning to make me feel like my heart will burst. I just want to cry."

S: "Good. Let your heart break. Let go of the suffering that keeps you back from life. Do you hear yourself now? Your heart is so open and the pain is right there. You are doing now just what you need to do—to just feel with so much compassion for yourself what you are going through.

"There is no rush to this process of opening, there is no emergency. Just slowly begin to make room in your heart for yourself. Perhaps tonight you will sit down with your daughter and feel that pain and just share it with her."

Feeling the Pain

We spoke of the resistance to life which filters every perception, which pushes away our connectedness with all that we love and leaves us feeling so isolated. And I encouraged her to just start to breathe in to her heart with whatever love might mean to her at that moment and to breathe it back out, to send it to her daughter. To allow herself to move into her experience and not hold back. That her essential connectedness with her daughter would become apparent beyond the ancient barricades which had so often kept her separate from the moment. "Let your pain be there and open around it. Open so that you can feel her pain and your pain together. You know, if pain made a sound, the atmosphere would be humming all the time. What you are sharing with your daughter now is being shared by tens of thousands of other beings at this very moment. Let it be in love instead of fear. Let her death be surrounded by your care for her and a willingness to go beyond your fear. To open to her death in a kind of new birth shared now for you both."

D: "I can't talk much now, my chest hurts so, but in my heart I hear my daughter saying 'thank you.'"

Before Dorothy's daughter died, they had many long "midnight talks" about her father's and brothers' deaths. Dorothy said at first she was "terribly uncomfortable bringing this all up" but that it seemed to put her daughter more at ease. "We talked at length about cancer and God. And I told her I loved her in a way that even losing her could not diminish. I don't think I have ever acknowledged my feelings to anyone so directly. It felt terrible. It felt wonderful."

> *"We must take care not to formalize or prescribe the way in which people express emotion."*

Open Grieving May Not Be Necessary

Norman Klein

Norman Klein is professor of anthropology at California State University in Los Angeles. In the following viewpoint, Klein expresses his belief that current theories place excessive emphasis on going through a grieving process. Different cultures and individuals react differently to death, he argues, and society should not place a single standard on how to grieve.

As you read, consider the following questions:

1. What "faddish" therapies does Klein describe for resolving grief? What does he think is wrong with them?
2. What differences does the author see in the way cultural groups react to death?
3. What does the author believe are the new myths and stereotypes of death?

Norman Klein, "Is There a Right Way to Die?" Reprinted with permission, from *Psychology Today* magazine, October 1978. Copyright 1978, Ziff-Davis Publishing Company.

In our own society, faddish therapies stress the idea that openly expressing sorrow, anger, or pain is a good thing, and the only means for "dealing with one's feelings honestly." "Holding things in" comes to be seen as deviant.

Yet nowhere has it been convincingly proved that expressing grief has universal therapeutic value. Perhaps more important, this insistence on the requirement to feel and tell represents an ethnocentric standard that can do injustice to persons and groups who cope differently.

Grief and Denial

Americans are said to fear and deny death, and if the denial becomes complete, it requires "defenses which can only be destructive," in the words of Elisabeth Kübler-Ross. She is perhaps best known for her scheme of the five stages of a "complete" death: (1) denial, (2) anger, (3) bargaining, (4) depression, and (5) acceptance. Each stage has a transitional value—taken alone, for instance, denial is seen as bad, though as a temporary buffer it is good—and, given enough time, a patient can reach a point of accepting death. Kübler-Ross's work is undoubtedly useful; it may even help family, friends, and professionals to assist the dying patient who has the emotional needs she describes. Yet it is surely conceivable that some Americans can work through grief internally or privately, without psychological cost; it is even more conceivable that whole cultural subgroups may have different ways of conceiving and responding to such experience. Harvard psychiatrist Ned H. Cassem has questioned the generally negative view of denial espoused by Kübler-Ross. "Denial can be a constructive force, enabling people to put out of mind morbid, frightening, and depressing aspects of life."

Standards May Be Arbitrary

A cross-cultural perspective reveals how arbitrary any one such standard may be. In 1976, psychologists Paul Rosenblatt, Patricia Walsh, and Douglas Jackson used the Human Relations Area Files, a massive compendium of anthropological data, to examine mourning in a large number of societies. They found in their review of 73 societies that what varies is the form and intensity of its expression. In 72 societies, people weep at death; the Balinese say they laugh to avoid crying. Are the Balinese unhealthy? The researchers also correlated gender differences in crying for 60 societies: in 32 of them, both sexes cried equally; in the 28 in which there was a difference, it was always the women who cried more. Are they healthier?

In 18 of 32 societies, self-injury (such as cutting off a finger at a joint) is regularly attempted by both grieving men and women; women self-mutilate more in 12. But if emotional letting go is a good thing, should men and women, equally, mutilate themselves even more frequently?

Closer to home, psychologist Richard Kalish and anthropologist David Reynolds compared the attitudes on death and mourning of black Americans, Japanese-Americans, Mexican-Americans, and white Americans in Los Angeles. Asked if they would "try very hard to control the way you showed your emotions in public," the groups offered a wide range of responses. Japanese and black respondents said they would (82 percent, 79 percent) more often than white Americans and Mexican-Americans, for example (74 percent, 64 percent).

Different Cultural Responses to Death

Death is an event occurring in all societies, yet it evokes an incredible variety of responses. At the moment of death, survivors in some societies remain rather calm, some cry, while others mutilate their own bodies. Some societies officially mourn for months, yet others complete the ritual within hours. Family involvement in preparation of the corpse for the funeral ritual exists in many societies, while others call professional funeral directors to handle the job.

The variety of responses to death is further noted by Richard Huntington and Peter Metcalf in *Celebrations of Death: The Anthropology of Mortuary Ritual*. They state that corpses are burned or buried, with or without animal or human sacrifice; they are preserved by smoking, embalming, or pickling; they are eaten—raw, cooked, or rotten; they are ritually exposed as dead or decaying flesh or simply abandoned; they are first dismembered and treated in a variety of ways. Funerals are times for avoiding people or holding parties, for weeping or laughing, for combat or sexual orgies.

George Dickinson, *Understanding Dying, Death, and Bereavement*, 1990.

Japanese-Americans, who are most frequently reticent about public grief, would seem to bear out the stereotypic notion of Orientals as stoic. Public-health nurse Thelma Dobbins Payne reports that the reluctance of many Japanese-American women to cry out during childbirth leads some non-Japanese physicians to "wonder if Japanese women feel the pain." Japanese-American physicians, however, described a common alternative style in labor: "wincing," "grimacing," "frowning." How much and what type of emoting is necessary to avoid the label "stoic"? The real issue rests with the way the various cultures define the appropriate expression of emotion. At the same time, it is very important to note that in no group Kalish and Reynolds studied

153

was there a 100 percent agreement by all informants—sex, age, religion, and education all affected the responses.

"Death with dignity" and "a beautiful death" verge on becoming the new jargon of concern. But for whom are these expressions really meaningful? Do they describe the dying person's experience, or the observer's? Attitudes toward death are clearly influenced by culture—and by subculture, and by individual personality. It follows, then, that we must take care not to formalize or prescribe the way in which people express emotion. As Kalish and Reynolds remark in their discussion, "This era is in danger of replacing old myths and stereotypes with new myths and stereotypes, slightly more accurate and less destructive perhaps, but nonetheless not always appropriate."

"A sincere expression of caring—and sharing— can help us to turn the grief of futility and despair into the grief of faith and hope and release."

Friends Can Help the Grieving Cope with Death

Barbara Russell Chesser

Hearing of a friend's or relative's loss sends many people into an agonizing dilemma of their own. Not wishing to offend the grieving person, friends may avoid the situation, fearing that what they say or do could be the wrong thing. In the following viewpoint, Barbara Russell Chesser, a writer, insists that virtually anything a friend does will help the grieving person. She describes five concrete ways a friend can help.

As you read, consider the following questions:

1. Why does Chesser believe it is important for the grieving person to see and hear from friends?
2. What does the author mean when she says friends should listen to the grieving person?
3. What, according to Chesser, is the one *wrong* thing a friend can say to a grieving person?

Barbara Russell Chesser, "How to Comfort Those Who Grieve," *Reader's Digest*, April 1986. Reprinted with permission.

The phone call came like a hammer blow. "Both of Gail Simone's parents were killed last night in a car crash." The caller was W. J. Wimpee, chaplain of Baylor University in Waco, Texas. He knew that Gail, a student, was a friend of mine. When I heard what had happened, a terrible numbness set in. *What can I do to help?*

This age-old question arises whenever a relative, friend or colleague suffers a death in the family. Like me that day, most people are at a loss to know how to respond. Trying to find some answers, I later talked with Chaplain Wimpee.

"Many people are immobilized out of fear they'll do or say the wrong thing," he said. Obviously, there is no one dramatic gesture or pearl of wisdom that will dissolve the heartache, but there are many acts of thoughtfulness that can convey your concern and help to soften the blow that a friend or loved one has suffered. From Wimpee and other experts on bereavement, here are five ways to say "I care."

1. Be there. Fran Philips was a real-estate agent in New York City. During an especially busy winter period, Fran's mother died. The funeral was to be held in Bel Air, Md., that weekend, and Helen, Fran's boss, would have to handle Fran's work on top of her own.

Helen was warmly sympathetic, and insisted that Fran leave for Bel Air right away. Heavy snows were forecast. "If you hurry," Helen said, "you might beat the weather." Two days later, as Fran was greeting her mother's friends after services at the chapel, Helen came up quietly behind her. She had driven all night through a snowstorm. "Why stay in New York," Helen asked, "when all my thoughts were here with you?"

Going to the Funeral

For years, Chuck Grayson, an insurance man in Lexington, Ky., avoided funerals. "I didn't think it made much difference whether I went or not," he recalls. "But when my wife died, I saw how many friends and relatives made a special effort to be at her funeral. Suddenly I knew how important this is to the person who has suffered the loss."

It is just as important to go to the bereaved person's home. "I don't remember anything that was said," my mother recalls of the period after my father died, when well-wishers flocked to her home. "What I *do* remember are those heartfelt hugs."

By being there, you can help in other ways. John DeFrain, a social researcher at the University of Nebraska, has studied about 500 families who have experienced unexpected death. "At first," he says, "they are so stunned they don't even know what *they* need to do, let alone tell others how to help." This is why people who are grief-struck seldom respond to the well-meaning offer, "if there is anything I can do, let me know."

Even a government agency like NASA recognizes the importance of being there. Following the fire and explosion that destroyed the *Challenger* space shuttle in January [1986], the families of each of the seven astronauts who were lost had another astronaut family at their side soon after the disaster. The support families were there to help the *Challenger* families with everything from travel and food arrangements to boarding the family pet. "With the vast technology of our space age," says Clarke Covington, manager of the Space-Station Project at NASA's Johnson Space Center in Houston, "there's still nothing more powerful than one human being reaching out to another."

A Letter to a Friend

Please dear friend
Don't say to me the old clichés
Time heals all wounds
God only gives you as much as you can bear
Life is for the living . . .
Just say the thoughts of your heart
I'm sorry, I love you, I'm here, I care
Hug me and squeeze my hand
I need your warmth and strength.

Please don't drop your eyes when I am near
I feel so rejected now by God and man
Just look in my eyes and let me know that you are with me.

Don't think you must always be strong for me
It's okay to cry
It tells me how much you care
Let me cry, too
It's so lonely to always cry alone.

Please keep coming by even after many weeks have passed
When the numbness wears off the pain of grief is unbearable.
Don't ever expect me to be quite the same
How can I be when part of my being is here no more.

But please know, dear friend, with your love, support and
understanding
I will live and love again and be grateful every day
                              that I have you—dear friend.

Mary Bailey

Elaine Vail, *A Personal Guide to Living with Loss.* New York: John Wiley & Sons, 1982. Reprinted with permission.

---

2. Listen. "One month after their high-school graduation, two boys were killed in an accident," says Bob Johns, youth pastor of a church in Woodway, Texas. "I visited both sets of parents, and we talked about the weather, our jobs—everything but their sons." Johns had felt he should never intrude on privacy and grief.

Then he heard a speaker from Compassionate Friends, a national organization that helps parents cope with the death of a child. The speaker's son had died. "She said no one would talk about him. Her greatest fear was that her son's short life would go unnoticed and unremembered." Johns began to realize that grieving people need to talk about this sudden vacuum in their lives.

A short time later, Johns encountered the father of one of the boys killed in the accident. After the usual amenities, Johns said, "Scott and I had a wonderful visit the last time I saw him." Immediately, the father's face lit up. "Really? What did he say?" Johns recounted their last conversation. "Then Scott's father started talking," says Johns, "and it was like a floodgate opening up."

What Not to Say

In a survey of bereaved people, 20 out of 25 felt most sympathizing comments didn't help and some actually hurt. Cited were such remarks as: "It's better now because he is at peace"; "Don't question God's purpose"; "You'll get over this." Above all, never say, "I know how you feel" unless you really have gone through the same experience.

The best way to get a mourner to open up is with a question: "Would you like to talk?" or "It must be hard to think about life without her; how are you adjusting?"

The need to listen and show grief extends to children, says Catherine Loughlin, retired professor of child development at the University of Nevada in Reno. When her husband died suddenly, their son, Martin, was six and daughter, Louise, only three. Loughlin said little to them about their father and returned to normal family routine as soon as possible. About six months later, Louise blurted, "Won't Daddy be surprised when he sees how I've grown!" Martin wrinkled his young brow. "Daddy is dead. Let's not talk about him ever again!"

Catherine Loughlin realized her children had been wrestling with the same painful emotions that she had been stifling. "When we began sharing our feelings," she says, "we finally began to accept the unacceptable."

3. *Send a note.* Julie, an honor student at the University of Nebraska and the only daughter of Clark and June Hudson, was hit by a truck and died. The Hudsons cherish a note from one of Julie's professors. "She wrote us," June says, "how much she had enjoyed having Julie in class, how cheerful and considerate she was and how much others liked her. It eased our misery to

know that she was remembered that way."

Notes can share personal memories or they can be simple and short, such as "I'm thinking of you during these painful days," or "I am praying for you during this time."

Helping Our Friends

The help of loving and supportive friends can be immensely valuable in the long and painful process of trying to build a new life without that special person whose loss seems insurmountable. But because we feel uneasy around those who are grieving, we usually spend less time with them at the precise period in their lives when they need us most. . . .

We can become a very useful and significant source of comfort for our friends who are bereaved. In our often fruitless search for the right thing to say, we frequently forget that there are lots of things that we can *do* to help our friends through a period of mourning and readjustment.

Elizabeth Ogg, *Facing Death and Loss*, 1985.

One of my friends wrote simply, "My prayer for you is a verse which meant a lot to me when my daughter died: 'Cast your burden on the Lord, and he will sustain you.' " (Psalm 55:22)

4. Give a gift. After Mary Christensen's 19-year-old daughter was killed in a motorcycle and car collision in Connecticut, she found solace in a collection of poems that a friend gave her. "She took special care in choosing something that would be meaningful to me," Mary says. "The poems put into words all the emotions I was feeling."

For years our neighbors had admired the beautiful flowers my grandfather grew. When he died, the neighbors gave the community library a book on flowering plants, in memory of Granddad. My grandmother was deeply moved.

Useful Books

Several widows I know received Helen Thames Raley's book *For Those Who Wait for Morning: Thoughts on Being a Widow* soon after their husbands died; and they, in turn, give the book to other new widows. *Tracks of a Fellow Struggler*, by John Claypool, may be helpful to parents who have lost a child. Other books that console include *When Bad Things Happen to Good People*, by Rabbi Harold Kushner; and *Don't Take My Grief Away*, by Doug Manning.

5. Extend an invitation. Kim Parker's mother died the summer Kim turned 17. "It was one week before my birthday," she recalls. "At the end of every summer, Mom and I had always

159

combined my birthday with shopping for school clothes. It was our special day together." Kim's friend Cari knew this. "So on the morning of the first birthday after my mother died," Kim says, "Cari called and asked if I would like to go shopping for school clothes. This was the most thoughtful thing anyone could have done."

An invitation gives the bereaved something to look forward to—instead of looking back on the source of pain and suffering. Consider what the person likes to do: Eat out? Go to plays? Take a drive? A friend of mine remembers that during the first few days after her husband's funeral, even a simple trip to the supermarket was difficult. "Now I always ask a new widow to let me go with her to the grocery store," she says.

Bereaved people often decline invitations—or accept only to cancel at the last minute. "People in deep mourning may fear losing control of their emotions in front of others," says Paul Stripling, executive director of the Waco Baptist Association. "They may even feel that if they have a good time, they are being disloyal to the person's memory." Gentle encouragement, he says, "will help them know it's all right to begin enjoying life again."

The death of a loved one is a devastating emotional loss. But a sincere expression of caring—and sharing—can help us to turn the grief of futility and despair into the grief of faith and hope and release.

> *"The intolerance of family and friends for those grieving a deceased spouse . . . is more the rule than the exception."*

Friends May Harm the Grieving Process

Ira Nerken

Ira Nerken is an attorney and director of Widowed Persons Grieving Support Groups, a self-help organization based in Washington, D.C. In the following viewpoint, he argues that people who are grieving are often harmed by their friends and relatives who do not comprehend their pain and anger. Friends' efforts to soften grief often harm the people they are trying to help, Nerken asserts. Grief, he argues, is an essentially private affair that friends and relatives can only partially understand.

As you read, consider the following questions:

1. What is disrespectful about many people's attempts to help a grieving friend, according to Nerken?
2. What are some examples of inappropriate things told the grieving person, according to the author?

Ira Nerken, "Making It Safe to Grieve." Copyright 1988, Christian Century Foundation. Reprinted, with permission, from *The Christian Century*, November 30, 1988.

I'm so ashamed," the young widow told me over the phone, weeping softly. She had called about a self-help support group I lead for the young newly widowed. Her husband had died of cancer at 38, after only three years of marriage.

Her tears were occasioned not by the pain of her horrible loss, sharpened by the shortness of the marriage, nor even the ubiquitous fears for the future that stalk the newly bereaved. The shame, embarrassment, and humiliation she and others speak of, the "feeling that there's something wrong with me," arose from her inability to stop grieving, no matter how much those around her told her she should.

Her parents and friends, she said, had grown impatient with her crying and her incessant talking about (and often to) her dead husband. She wanted to accommodate them, but the tears kept flowing, the "obsessing" continued and she saw no hope of it ending soon.

Given her mother's and father's exasperation, I wondered how long it had been since her husband died. Painfully she admitted it had been "over three months." *Three months.* "There is nothing wrong with you," I gently kidded her, "but I'd check out your parents."

Intolerance of Family and Friends

The intolerance of family and friends for those grieving a deceased spouse—even for those who have lost their spouse in the first years of marriage—is more the rule than the exception. Parents, friends, relatives, clergy, and counselors who offer support to the bereaved in the first weeks or months after the death soon begin finding "subtle but effective ways," as Douglas Manning puts it, "to take grief away." A mother asks a grieving offspring if the crying "really helps." Friends suggest that it's "time to move on." Neighbors take the new widow aside—sometimes only minutes after the funeral—and counsel her to "be strong," as though to grieve were weak.

William Sloane Coffin has talked of the reactions he encountered from some fellow ministers during his first months of grief over the drowning death of his teenage son. Many offered "comforting words of Scripture" to suggest he find God's will or some blessing in the midst of tragedy. But "the reality of grief is the absence of God," he noted, and we must guard against words offered "for self-protection, to pretty up a situation whose bleakness [we] simply [cannot] face. . . ." Such attempts to soften grief show no regard for the magnitude of the loss the bereaved are feeling, at a time when they are sensitive to any suggestion that their grief may be exaggerated.

While efforts to reduce someone's grieving may seem justified as acts of love, and motivated only by a wish to minimize another's pain (and thus are difficult, especially for the bereaved, to challenge), they fail the first test of love: they do not show respect. To assert that we know better than the griever, particularly one who is in a situation we cannot possibly comprehend, how she should feel, think, or behave is fundamentally disrespectful. Normally we would not so presume or condescend, knowing it to be wrong and fearing the other's reaction.

"Sometimes a cute card just isn't appropriate, Jane."

Many people, however, consider the bereaved's situation pathetic, her tears signs of helplessness, and her distress evidence of weakness and confusion. Such an attitude leads normally loving people to violate the griever's self-respect and dignity. While their actions may leave the griever "wondering if [she is] weak or even crazy," Manning notes, they are sure they know better than the griever what is right for her, for they aren't in as much pain.

The notion that people experiencing intense emotional pain don't quite know what they are doing (or they wouldn't be doing it) is the root problem leading to disrespect for grief and the griever. It is based on a belief, as firmly held as it is wrongheaded, that expressing so much pain is neither necessary nor constructive. Once you believe that the pain of grief is needless, it is hard to appreciate a process that is putting your loved one through such pain. And if one assumes that the pain is unnecessary, it is hard to appreciate your loved ones for putting *you* through it.

While Manning ascribes such hostility to general ignorance about grief's stages (shock, tears, anger), it rests rather on prejudices toward the pain that are capable of withstanding considerable education about the grief cycle. Once the extraordinary intensity and longevity of grief's pain is actually witnessed, many people (including not a few grievers) simply refuse to believe that an emotional response of this magnitude could possibly be healthy, or be what grieving books, counselors, etc., are referring to ("They told me you'd cry, but not *this* much!"). It is also hard to imagine a purpose great enough to justify something so terrible to bear—or to watch.

Those who hope to help the bereaved must respect her pain and accept the fact that it is necessary and vital. While suppressing tears, ruminations, and painful feelings may expedite the bereaved's effort to "function normally," it hinders the process of working through the loss. Acknowledging and expressing the pain helps the griever recover her sense of self and renew her sense of meaning and purpose so that she can again truly and joyously embrace life, though the love of one's life is gone.

The self-healing process of reinterpreting and reintegrating the meaning of one's life and love cannot be rushed, but it can easily be waylaid. The griever will experience a variety of feelings, and needs to hear from loving supporters: "Feel whatever you are feeling; I am listening and learning; I admire your courage." This encouragement affirms the grief process at a time when the slightest criticism can send it under cover, and offers certainty in the midst of doubt: this *is* the way to recovery. Those who speak impatiently to the griever are subtle collaborators in death's message, and it is important for them to realize it. Their refusal to concede any meaning or purpose to the griever's thoughts and feelings confirms that all that she once cherished *is* lost, irretrievably; what love now leads her to do will lead nowhere. Leave it alone, many say; time heals all wounds. But a shattered life is never fully recovered without work. . . .

A Conversation with the Self

Grief is, in fact, an extended conversation—with others, but primarily with the self. If grief is not suppressed, the griever eventually persuades the part of the self that fears it must stay behind—out of love for the one now dead—that the loved one's meaning and purpose is best preserved, albeit in new form, only if it will let go. In this conversation, it very much matters that the griever talk to herself respectfully. When those around her declare that "tears won't bring him back," "no one needs to hear the story again," or more innocuously suggest that she best "cheer up," the griever may repeat these fatuous messages to herself, making her grief a kind of banal self-chastisement. . . .

When the pain and anger of grief are allowed to take their course, they will eventually join with the gamut of other feelings of grief, including joy and hope as well as sorrow, to focus on the true enemy, death, and the true goal, life. Recovery, after all, can be seen as life's bold act, affirming itself in angry defiance against death. The pain that leads to anger at the violation inflicted on one's meaning and purpose becomes the will to find a new meaning. Where death declared, "All is lost," grievers finally reply, "Not by a long shot," and go on to recover the very different, positive, and constructive meaning that lies waiting for each of us, whenever we choose life.

"From the hour of death until the deceased person's final disposition, a professional funeral director helps families through their time of crisis."

Professionally Arranged Funerals Can Help the Grieving

National Funeral Directors Association

Funerals are ceremonies held to commemorate the dead, often held just before or during the burial or cremation of the body. The following viewpoint, taken from a pamphlet produced by the National Funeral Directors Association, explains the importance of funerals in helping survivors cope with their grief, and emphasizes the importance of funeral directors in helping families arrange the funeral of a family member. The NFDA is a federation of funeral directors' associations. It provides professional education seminars and publishes numerous pamphlets on death and dying.

As you read, consider the following questions:

1. How do funerals enable survivors to come to terms with the death of a loved one, according to the NFDA?
2. What services do professional funeral directors provide, according to the authors?
3. How does the NFDA compare funeral directors and physicians?

Reprinted by permission of the National Funeral Directors Association from its 1988 brochure "Yes, Funerals Are for the Living."

It is never easy to accept death. After hearing that a loved one has died, we may feel angry, confused or emotionally numb. We may not know how to express our feelings of loss, or how to say good-bye to the person who has died.

But we do need to work through these feelings, and that's what makes a funeral so important. A funeral is a ritual that can help focus our emotions and bring meaning to the experience of death.

The Function of Rituals

"Rituals link us with the past and the future," explains Dr. Judith Stillion, a professor of psychology at Western Carolina University. "We have rituals for graduations and marriages, and we need a ritual for this most important passage of life."

The funeral serves as a means to commemorate the deceased, but, just as importantly, it helps the survivors to heal emotionally. When someone we love dies, we experience the pain of grief. But even though it hurts, grief is not something to avoid. Grief is part of the healing process that allows us to separate ourselves from the deceased person and go on with our lives.

A funeral gives mourners ritual "permission" to express feelings of sadness and loss. Funerals also stimulate mourners to begin talking about the deceased, one of the first steps toward accepting the death. In fact, people who do not attend the funeral of a loved one because they want to deny the death may suffer from unresolved grief several months later.

To resolve their grief, mourners need to accept the reality of death not only on an intellectual level, but on an emotional level as well. It is for this reason that funerals in our culture are usually preceded by an open-casket visitation period.

Dr. Stillion says she used to feel that viewings were a barbaric custom. But her research into grief has changed her mind. "Nothing helps you accept the death as much as seeing the dead person," she said. "It helps with grieving because it shows that there's no return."

The Role of a Funeral Director

A death in the family burdens family members with grief and disrupts their normal lives. With everything else, these mourners may not want the additional responsibility of thinking through and then planning and coordinating all the details of the funeral. Fortunately, they don't have to. From the hour of death until the deceased person's final disposition, a professional funeral director helps families through their time of crisis. The funeral director is the one person who, at various times, serves as advisor, administrator, supporter and caregiver.

When the funeral director is called after a person dies, one of his initial responsibilities is to bring the deceased person's body to the funeral home. He also secures information for the deceased person's death certificate, which he then completes and files with the proper legal authorities.

Reprinted by permission of Johnny Hart and NAS, Inc.

The funeral director meets with the family to discuss arrangements for a visitation, if the family requests one, and a funeral. In accordance with law, custom and especially the family's wishes, the funeral director helps them make choices that meet their needs. These choices may include a traditional funeral service and visitation, a memorial service without the body present or immediate disposition.

A Source of Information

Should the family choose to have some type of service, the funeral director helps them choose the place and time for a service and the clergyperson or other person who will preside at the service. He also provides information to help the family choose a casket or other burial container, a memorial stone or appropriate marker and the means of final disposition—usually burial, cremation or entombment.

On the day of the funeral, the funeral director attends to a number of ceremonial and administrative details, as well as to logistical matters such as transportation. Both before and after the service, the funeral director helps the family complete necessary paperwork, including obituary notices, claim forms for social security, veteran's and union benefits, and insurance. Because the emotional impact of death often makes it difficult to concentrate on the details of legal forms, the funeral director's help in this area is especially appreciated by grieving families.

The funeral director's role, of course, is not limited to logistics and paperwork. He is also ready to help families work through any concerns they may have resolving their grief. Today's funeral director is trained to answer questions about coping with death, to recognize when a person is having difficulty accepting the loss of a loved one and to recommend sources of professional counseling for those who need it.

Many funeral directors play an active role as caregivers outside the funeral home. They may be involved with nursing facilities, hospices, and with self-help groups such as The Compassionate Friends and Widow-to-Widow. In essence, the funeral director's role in serving bereaved people is similar to the general medical practitioner's role in serving the ill: Taking care of their basic needs, and helping guide them to specialists when extra care is required.

"Handling and transporting the body, gathering the paperwork, and making all other arrangements gave me control in a way that was therapeutic."

Family-Arranged Funerals Can Help the Grieving

Lisa Carlson

In 1981 Lisa Carlson arranged the funeral of her husband without the use of a funeral director. In the following viewpoint, she concludes from that experience that such funerals, arranged by family and community members, are much more meaningful than funerals provided by professionals who do not personally know the deceased person. Carlson is the author of the book *Caring for Your Own Dead.*

As you read, consider the following questions:

1. What was the original reason Carlson decided not to use a professional funeral director?
2. Why does the author believe professionally arranged funerals may be emotionally unsatisfying?
3. According to Carlson, why did embalming become part of many U.S. funerals?

From "Caring for Our Own Dead" by Lisa Carlson, in *Woman of Power*, "Life Cycles: Conscious Birthing, Living, and Dying," Issue #14, Summer 1989. Reprinted with permission. (Carlson's book, *Caring for Your Own Dead* may be ordered by calling 1-800-356-9315.)

In 1981, after the death of my husband, I handled his burial arrangements without the use of a funeral director. That was considered unusual at the time.

I had initially made the decision for financial reasons. In addition to the grief of a sudden death, as a new widow I faced an immediate need to take over as the sole breadwinner for my children. There was not enough money in the bank for the next grocery shopping, let alone the thousands of dollars a "traditional" funeral would cost.

A Therapeutic Experience

As it turned out, the experience provided benefits that were more important than just saving money. The need to remain in control of the physical events helped me to avoid falling apart emotionally. Handling and transporting the body, gathering the paperwork, and making all other arrangements gave me control in a way that was therapeutic. It made me feel less helpless. If I had simply turned the body over to strangers, I would have had a much harder time accepting the reality of John's untimely death. There was no bargaining with God to wake up a pink and powdered lifelikeness.

Often, funeral professionals can provide help that is needed and welcome. Not everyone is inclined—or even able—to build a casket, transport a body, or even, at a time of grief, assemble the information needed for a death certificate or an obituary.

Unfortunately, the role of the funeral industry has gone beyond that of providing help, at a fair price, at a time of need. In all too many instances, funeral directors take over all arrangements. One of several standard packages is chosen, and the family writes the check. If the cost is $5,000, then the deceased gets the $5,000 deal. Relationships that are lovingly complex during life become reduced to package deals at a time of death.

As a society, we've lost the knowledge of caring for our own dead. People feel that they are unable to do anything for a departed friend except spend money. So they spend as much money as they can, and then, after the event, feel unfulfilled as well as broke.

It wasn't always that way, of course. In early America, home funerals were the practice everywhere. Each community had a group of women who came in to help "lay out the dead." Last respects were paid in the homes of family members and in church.

Even today in some parts of this country, religious and ethnic groups have maintained the practice of caring for their own. A funeral director is sometimes called in as a helper, but support groups and family are in control. Native Americans, the Amish, and Quakers, for example, often provide emotional support for a

171

grieving family and actively participate in funeral arrangements.

The funeral industry was organized in the late 1800s and began promoting its members as sophisticated professionals. The centerpiece of its promotional efforts was the practice of embalming, which until that time was considered to be an outdated, exotic custom of the ancient Egyptians. Embalming had one advantage—it preserved bodies for later viewings when refrigeration was not available. It was also promoted as a means of "sanitation"—to prevent the spread of disease. That theory has long since been discredited, but the mythology about embalming has persisted in the United States. Unlike any other country in the world, in the United States embalming is still an "expected" part of the majority of funeral arrangements.

Home Funerals

In early America, home funerals were the practice everywhere, and each community had a group of women who came in to help with the "laying out of the dead." Visitation was held in the front parlor followed by a procession to the church and cemetery. . . .

In some parts of North America, religious and ethnic groups have maintained the practice of caring for their own dead. With the spread of the hospice movement, families are assuming more responsibility at the time of death, and home or church funerals are again returning. Those who have been involved with such funerals have found them therapeutic and meaningful, with costs being minimal.

Continental Association of Funeral and Memorial Societies, "Earth Burial," 1991.

Embalming requires expertise and equipment. Once families and support groups were convinced to turn to the professionals for embalming, it was a simple next step to start depending on professionals for all other aspects of funeral arrangements. Generations of Americans lost the knowledge of how to care for their dead and became completely dependent upon professionals.

To some extent, people are willing victims of the funeral industry. The fact is, in 41 states a family (or a support group with the consent of the family) has the right to handle all death arrangements without the use of a funeral director. In all states, families and friends can take on at least some of the duties usually assigned to a funeral home, if they can find a funeral director who is willing to work with them. If they choose not to do so, the decision is theirs.

Now I think that a quiet revolution is beginning, one that may gradually change what Jessica Mitford termed "the American way of death" in her influential book of the same name. People are beginning to question whether the best way to say good-bye to a person they love is to shell out big bucks for a funeral. Some are reasserting their rights to control the ways they say good-bye.

If a funeral means anything at all, it is an affirmation of our connections with each other. The person who died was, and is, part of our own lives. Handling funeral arrangements for a friend is a deeply emotional experience. It forces us to think about our spiritual relationships, and to put into perspective our physical relationships.

a critical thinking activity

Coping with Grief

The viewpoints in this chapter discuss the grieving process and how others might help or hinder that process. In this exercise you will examine your own past experiences with grief, and use those experiences to learn about the grieving process.

Part I

Each member of the class should try to remember the death of a close relative, friend, or pet. Then answer the following questions.

1. What feelings did you experience after the death?
2. How did you handle your grief? Describe activities or conversations that were beneficial in helping you grieve.
3. How did other people help you overcome your grief? What were the most helpful things said to you? What were the least helpful?
4. If you attended a funeral or other ceremony, did that help you with your grief? Why or why not?
5. Using your experience, how would you counsel a friend who is grieving?

Part II

The class should form into groups of four to six students. Students should then discuss their answers to the questions in Part I.

Part III

Each group or the entire class should complete the following sentences.

1. The most common characteristics of people who are grieving are _____.

2. The three most helpful things I can do or say for a friend who is grieving are _____.

3. The three worst things I can do or say for a friend who is grieving are _____.

Periodical Bibliography

The following articles have been selected to supplement the diverse views presented in this chapter.

Barbara Baumgardner   "When a Friend Grieves," *Moody Monthly*, March 1992. Available from PO Box 2062, Marion, OH 43305-2062.

Sandra Butler   "A Mother's Lament," *Utne Reader*, September/October 1991.

Diane Cole   "Grief's Lessons: His and Hers," *Psychology Today*, December 1988.

John Deedy   "Widow's Might: How to Build a New Life When a Spouse Dies," *U.S. Catholic*, March 1988.

Monica Dickens   "When I Lost My Husband," *Reader's Digest*, March 1987.

Stephanie Ericsson   "The Agony of Grief," *Utne Reader*, September/October 1991.

David Gelman et al.   "The Cruelest Kind of Grief," *Newsweek*, January 2, 1989.

L. Gregory Jones   "Giving Voice to the Silences," *The Christian Century*, April 11, 1990.

Joanne Kaufman   "My Mother Died Too Soon," *Glamour*, November 1989.

Donald W. McCullough   "Why You Don't Have to Cheer Up," *Christianity Today*, November 5, 1990.

Geri Hess Mitsch   "Allowing Children to Grieve," *St. Anthony Messenger*, November 1991.

Daniel O'Hara   "Saying Farewell Honestly," *Free Inquiry*, Summer 1990. Available from PO Box 5, Buffalo, NY 14215-0005.

Malcolm P. Rogers and Peter Reich   "On the Health Consequences of Bereavement," *The New England Journal of Medicine*, August 25, 1988.

Anne Rosen   "Sweet Sorrow," *Ms.*, November 1989.

Sean P. Ryan   "Physicians and Funerals," *Journal of the American Medical Association*, March 4, 1992. Available from the American Medical Association, 515 N State St., Chicago, IL 60610.

Henry Seiden   "How Sharing Grief Can Ease the Pain," *U.S. News & World Report*, January 30, 1989.

Catherine Thompson and Barbara E. Moore   "Grief Is Not a Sign of Weakness," *USA Today*, July 1991.

Tim Unsworth   "Let Laypeople Have the Last Word," *U.S. Catholic*, August 1991.

Is There Life After Death?

DEATH≋DYING

Chapter Preface

Scientists excavating burial sites of prehistoric humans have found evidence of food, tools, and animal skins that many believe were to be used as provisions for the world beyond. If true, this would show that humans have had a belief in some sort of life after death for tens of thousands of years. Belief in life after death remains strong to this day. Recent surveys indicate that more than 70 percent of Americans eighteen and over believe in some sort of afterlife.

Opinions about life after death can be separated roughly into three categories. Some people believe that after death a person resides in a joyful paradise or an endless hell, to reward or punish the type of life the person led on earth. Beliefs of this sort are typical of Christianity, Judaism, and Islam. Other people believe in reincarnation—the belief that a person lives and dies many times and after each death is reborn into another body. This is a common belief in the Eastern religions of Hinduism and Buddhism. Finally, there are some who believe there is no existence after death, and beliefs in heaven or reincarnation are wishful thinking by people who refuse to accept the finality of death.

The question of life after death has traditionally been a religious and philosophical debate, not a scientific one. Because scientists rely solely on testing provable and observable phenomena, they have been unable to examine the question of life after death. In recent years, however, a growing number of researchers have investigated near-death experiences (NDEs). In NDEs, clinically "dead" people who have been revived relate experiences that are eerily similar and that many believe may prove the existence of an afterlife. Other people dismiss NDEs as hallucinations. The viewpoints in this chapter examine NDEs and other aspects of the eternal question: Is there life after death?

"We must rid ourselves of the debilitating and despairing dogma that death is an . . . absolutely final condition."

Human Consciousness May Survive Death

William A. Reinsmith

Whether or not humans maintain a conscious existence on some other plane after death is a question that has been debated by scientists and philosophers. In the following viewpoint, William A. Reinsmith argues that science has no way of determining for certain whether death is the ultimate end of human identity, and that there may be a spiritual dimension in which people live after death. By being open to this possibility, people will fear death less and live life more fully, he concludes. Reinsmith is a professor of humanities at the Philadelphia College of Pharmacy and Science.

As you read, consider the following questions:

1. How has science constricted our view of death, according to Reinsmith?
2. What two conditions are necessary to maintain a state of openness to the possibility of life after death, according to the author?
3. What does Reinsmith mean by spiritual humanism?

Adapted from William A. Reinsmith, "The Finality of Death: The Underlying Issue." Reprinted by permission of the publisher, *Humane Medicine*, vol. 5, 1989.

Numerous critics within and without the medical establishment have asked whether, in our technological age, the age-old ethic of preserving life has metamorphosed into a need to control life, to let no scent of death intrude—especially in our decision making. However, the deeper issue, which sets rigid limits to the debate, is not the need to master death or the refusal to acknowledge its existence, but rather technological society's belief in the utter finality of death.

An Alternative

In his book *Beyond the Post-Modern Mind*, Huston Smith points out that science does not prove that higher realms of being do not exist. Rather, it concentrates so completely on the physical, material aspects of existence that other aspects of the universe— aspects that for centuries provided a meaning to life—have become unimportant and then completely forgotten. Smith argues that, in tailoring our thinking to meet the criteria of scientific "objectivity, prediction, number, and control, [we have] constricted our world view" and brought about alienation. In the light of this result, he says, "it seems only sensible to consider alternative guidelines—perhaps even opposite ones to get the matter in sharp relief."

One of these guidelines, for Smith, is to allow for the possibility of surprise in our questioning, to develop capacities for wonder and openness in our thought. Such a guideline might be applied to the dogma of the finality of death in the following manner: No one has ever proved that another state of existence lies beyond this life. However, only one fact is beyond doubt—that all of us die, that our present state of existence comes to an end. This alone is absolutely true. The rest is open to conjecture. Whether any other state of existence follows, whether as persons we endure beyond the grave, is simply not known—and probably cannot be known in any conventionally scientific way. This, however, is not the same thing as saying another state of existence is not possible.

Some may think that the question is of no importance or value because science cannot deal with it in a meaningful way. But if we respond thus, we engage in the fallacy Smith has described above, dismissing a profoundly human question on the grounds that human aspiration and experience must parallel the dogmas or even the intellectual method of a particular society. To do this is to deny the complexity of human concerns, and the multi-leveled richness of human existence.

What is the most reasonable position in the face of such uncertainty? Would it not be an *openness* to the question? I believe society resists death so intensely because it is convinced of its utter finality. Given the lack of evidence either way, this position is unreasonable, and we need to bring our unreason into the open. Twenty-five hundred years ago, when asked if he was afraid of death, Socrates replied:

> No one knows with regard to death whether it is not really the greatest blessing that can happen to a man, but people dread it as though they were certain that it is the greatest evil, and this ignorance, which thinks it knows what it does not, must surely be ignorance most culpable.

There is great wisdom in this answer, as well as humility in the face of the unknown. It is the wisdom of a mind that had observed that life and death are coextensive—that we cannot have one without the other. In *The Broken Connection*, Robert Jay Lifton says that, in our modern age, we have lost not so much the theme of death as the "psychological relationship between the phenomenon of death and the flow of life."

"Norman, maybe it wasn't such a smart idea for you to have left everything to science."

Can we remain reasonable and open, as Socrates did in the face of his own death, or is it impossible for us to achieve such calm detachment in regard to the most important issue in life? In *Tragic Sense of Life*, Miguel De Unamuno argues that the specter of death is the ultimate threat to consciousness. Following Spinoza, he delineates the hunger for immortality as the essence of our being. By our very consciousness we long for more consciousness, and we cannot conceive its annihilation.

181

Therefore, we cannot maintain openness in such a condition. The stakes are too great. One way or the other, we must decide the question for ourselves, or else suppress all thoughts about the matter. Our modern age, with "scientific objectivity" as its beacon, seems to have opted against the possibility of anything after death. The issue, once decided, now lies forgotten by consciousness; yet fear of death is incredibly active underneath it and fuels the desire for life (this life) at any cost.

Implications

If openness is not possible, then a rational position involving a Socratic detachment in the face of death is a chimera. Furthermore, Socrates himself (or anyone else who spoke so) is not faithful to the psychological truth of human existence. To put the question most pointedly: Is it possible for a human consciousness to entertain the prospect of its own demise (or its possible continuance) with equanimity? I suggest, against De Unamuno, that such an openness may be consistent with the character of a well-lived life—and therefore wise.

Gabriel Marcel, the French phenomenologist, holds that such an openness is not only possible, but in keeping with "the structural aspects of the human being"—aspects that involve an "immersion in mystery." In "Mortality, Hope and Freedom," a chapter from *The Existential Background of Human Dignity*, he writes:

> Once more, unless one is the champion of a scientific materialism which seems to be plainly dated, I do not see how it can be seriously maintained that survival after death is purely and simply unthinkable. A margin of incertitude remains, and it is open to reflection as an aspect of the mystery involved in our destiny.

Marcel operates in an atmosphere of phenomenological openness that is the mark of a mature, spiritualized consciousness. In such a state—as opposed to the isolationism of a Sartrean position—something beyond death may be implied.

Again, I stress that this viewpoint "proves" nothing, but leaves a door open without being irrational. . . .

Scientific Corroboration

The scientific community also offers to corroborate openness to death. Sir John Eccles, commenting on his work with Karl Popper on the relationship between self and brain in "The Self-Conscious Mind and Meaning and Mystery of Personal Existence," points out that, from the standpoint of "dualistic interactionism," the death of the brain need not result in the destruction of the subjective self. All that can be inferred is that this self (or "programmer") ceases to have any relationship with the brain (the computer) and thus will lack all sensory information and all motor expression.

Eccles holds that there are great unknowns, not only in the material makeup and operation of our brains but also in the relationship of brain to mind, in our creative imagination, and in the uniqueness of the psyche:

> When we think of these unknowns as well as the unknown of how we came to be in the first place, we should be much more humble. The unimaginable future that could be ours would be the fulfillment of this our present life, and we should be prepared to accept its possibility as the greatest gift. In the acceptance of this wonderful gift of life and of death, we have to be prepared not for the inevitability of some other existence, but we can hope for the possibility of it.

If it is reasonable to hold a state of openness to the possibility of something beyond death, then we can exhibit equanimity in the face of death. However, such a state can be achieved only under two conditions.

Insufficient Imaginations

What happens after death is so unspeakably glorious that our imaginations and our feelings do not suffice to form even an approximate conception of it. . . .

Sooner or later, the dead all become what we also are. But in this reality, we know little or nothing about that mode of being. And what shall we still know of this earth after death? The dissolution of our time-bound form in eternity brings no loss of meaning. Rather, does the little finger know itself a member of the hand.

Carl Jung, quoted in "The Light Beyond," *New Age Journal*, May/June 1988.

First, one must cultivate a state of "Socratic ignorance" regarding what one knows. Huston Smith gives an example of what such ignorance implies. During a conversation, Robert Becker, a scientific neighbor doing research at New York's Upstate Medical Center, reflected, "We know nothing!" Smith assured him that he, too, was familiar with the skeptical tradition in Western philosophy. Becker replied, "That's not what I mean. It may be true generally, but it's especially true in medicine. Here I am, a director of medical research with 30 years behind me, and when I cut my face shaving I haven't any idea of what makes it heal."

In the light of such ignorance, Smith proposes that education should prepare us for *surprise* and must begin with the premise that, in comparison with what we do not know, we know nothing. This is what Socrates suggests in his reflections on death. I believe that only such an attitude can allow us to view death with dispassion and calm anticipation.

Second, we must be willing to "let go." When the controlling ego, immersed in a reductionist vision of reality formed by scientific positivism, will not loosen its grip, then any threat to that control is greeted with irrational denial or with spasms of fear—or even panic. But once the reins are relaxed and things are allowed to flow naturally, "what will be will be"—or, to put it in Buddhist terms, things will be allowed "to be what they are." Then the mind is at peace.

Tolstoy's "Death of Ivan Ilyich" provides the most powerful depiction in Western literature of this struggle to hold on. Ivan's death agony is intensified by his initial refusal not only to admit that he is dying but also to admit that his life of social conformity has been a moral failure. After a lengthy and terrific struggle, he gives in. At that moment the agony abates; finally, Ivan allows reality and truth to have their way.

> He sought his former accustomed fear of death and did not
> find it. "Where is it? What death?" There was no fear because
> there was no death. In place of death there was light.

Elisabeth Kübler-Ross, in *On Death and Dying*, describes at length how patients are able to arrive at a final stage in their dying where they let go and immediately achieve a kind of peace—"almost void of feelings": "It's as if the pain has gone, the struggle is over, and there comes time for 'the final rest before the long journey,' as one patient phrased it."

Beneficial Effects

The effects of such an openness to death could, I believe, be quite salutary. Overthrowing the social dogma of death's finality would release us from our obsession with materialism (and thus with physical existence alone), because we would now be more "unknowing" when confronted with the mystery of death. I suspect we would also get on much better with the business of living. Socrates believed that his main concern should be not with fleeing his impending death but with the importance of living a good life, one of "mental and moral well-being." All the great spiritual teachings corroborate this emphasis on living well and doing good. The symbolism and communal practices of the great religious traditions of the past nurtured this ability to live fully in the presence of death. When death is consciously accepted as inevitable, yet mysterious and open-ended, things fall into their proper perspective.

This done, we would be able to think differently about a number of bio-ethical dilemmas in our society today. Broadening the boundaries could allow us to entertain new perceptions and insights heretofore prevented by the societal dogma of "this life at all costs."

Indeed, our terror of the finality of death may be masking an opposite impulse. In *Heartsounds*, Hal and Martha Lear, like most of us, are quintessentially modern. Both railed against Hal's dying at 56. Yet, ironically, before his illness Hal never lived in a manner that would ensure his longevity. Because he came from a family with a history of heart disease, Hal was warned to live wisely with that knowledge. Yet for 30 years he smoked heavily, was a compulsive achiever, and chose to work in situations involving acute stress. Denial of death may actually produce a subconscious compulsion to bring it on—an existential despair veiled by a refusal to confront calmly the reality of an end to this present state of existence. Would such a confrontation be easier if one were to remain open, detached, and "uncaring" about the question? Would there be a confrontation at all? Or merely a meeting with the inevitable, and an attitude of quiet hope—which alone, Marcel claims, can cure the obsession with inevitable death and consequent lack of meaning.

Evidence for Life After Death

The sheer volume of physical evidence for survival after death is so immense that to ignore it is like standing at the foot of Mount Everest and insisting that you cannot see a mountain. This evidence is of many different types—accounts of near-death experiences, out-of-body experiences, and so on.

Colin Wilson in *What Survives?*, 1990.

Dylan Thomas's poem to his father, "Do not go gentle into that good night;/ Rage, rage against the dying of the light," is compelling, but it does not represent openness in the face of death. The words of Good Pope John, "Any day is a good day to be born; any day is a good day to die," while much more prosaic, have the wisdom of Zen sayings, which mask a profound simplicity and detachment in the face of the inevitable.

Finally, we need to distinguish prevailing scientific dogma— and its mechanistic, reductionist roots—from true science, which humbles itself before the unknown. In its original form, science was not a tool for mastery but rather an avenue for exploration of a universe we hardly suspect, much less know. It involved attitudes of openness, testing of hypotheses, and the use of metaphor. As Gregory Bateson puts it, in *Mind and Nature*, "Science, like all other methods of perception, is limited in its ability to collect the outward signs of whatever may be truth. Science *probes*; it does not prove." However, our need for certainty uses science and technology to shrink the dimensions of life to the merely measurable so that we might pretend to have absolute control.

185

Ours is a technological image of dying—antiseptic and sterile, not at all humane. Let us do what we can to change this reflection of a Brave New World. As teachers and caregivers, let us infuse a spiritual humanism into our relationships with our students and patients, one that finds that deep human center where openness to the transcendent is possible.

Spiritual humanism holds that, at the core of a human being, there is a spiritual dimension that can only be realized by reaching outward to others through openness and caring. In caring for others, one approaches the transcendent and, in doing so, becomes ever more human.

We should live with full awareness and die, when the time comes, with dignity and lightness, "in good spirits." In this way, our loved ones will not only be inspired to live well but be able to visualize their own deaths as a time of outreaching peace and openness. A caring society's task is to create conditions that render such a death not only possible but commonplace. Whatever technology we employ in terminal illness should be directed toward aiding "a good death": first, however, we must rid ourselves of the debilitating and despairing dogma that death is an unmitigated evil and absolutely final condition.

"It seems preposterous to assert that, when the brain is completely destroyed, the mind suddenly returns intact, with its emotional and intellectual capacities . . . restored."

Human Consciousness Does Not Survive Death

Paul Edwards

Paul Edwards teaches philosophy at Brooklyn College and the New School for Social Research in New York. His books include *Immortality*. In the following viewpoint, Edwards opposes the notion that human consciousness can continue to exist after death. He argues that the mind or consciousness of a person is dependent on the brain and its functions. When the brain perishes, Edwards concludes, the mind also dies.

As you read, consider the following questions:

1. What did Lucretius believe about the relationship between the body and the mind, according to the author?
2. How does Edwards use the example of Alzheimer's disease to disprove the existence of an afterlife?
3. How does Edwards define the word "soul"?

Paul Edwards, "The Case Against Reincarnation, Part III," *Free Inquiry*, Spring 1987. Reprinted with permission.

I now come to what seems to me the most important argument against survival after death in all its most familiar forms. I am in the habit of calling it "the body-mind dependence argument." The argument is already found in Lucretius, who stated the basic idea long before anything was known about the connection between consciousness and the brain:

> The understanding is begotten along with the body, and grows together with it, and along with it comes to old age. For as children totter with feeble and tender body, so a weak judgement of mind goes with it. Then when their years are ripe and their strength hardened, greater is their sense and increased their force of mind. Afterward, when now the body is shattered by the stern strength of time, and the frame has sunk with its force dulled, then the reason is maimed, the tongue raves, the mind stumbles, all things give way and fail at once. And so it is natural that all the nature of the mind should also be dissolved, even as is smoke, into the high breezes of the air; inasmuch as we see that it is born with the body, grows with it, and, as I have shown, at the same time becomes weary and worn with age.

The argument is found in Pomponazzi, Voltaire (who pretended to but did not in fact believe in immortality), Hume, Russell, Ayer, and numerous contemporary philosophers. It is stated very effectively, with specific reference to the dependence of conscious states on the brain, by J.J.C. Smart in the article on "Religion and Science" in *The Encyclopedia of Philosophy.* . . .

> Even if some form of philosophical dualism is accepted and the mind is thought of as something over and above the body, the empirical evidence in favor of an invariable correlation between mental states and brain states is extremely strong: that is, the mind may be thought of as in some sense distinct from the body but also as fundamentally dependent upon physical states. Without oxygen or under the influence of anesthetics or soporific drugs, we rapidly lose consciousness. Moreover, the quality of our consciousness can be influenced in spectacular ways by appropriate drugs or by mechanical stimulation of different areas of the brain. In the face of all the evidence that is being accumulated by modern research in neurology, it is hard to believe that after the dissolution of the brain there could be any thought or conscious experience whatever.

I will add one other recent formulation, which states the argument simply and forcefully and is based on the most recent evidence from neurology. "What we call 'the mind,'" writes Colin McGinn,

> is in fact made up of a great number of sub-capacities, and each of these depends upon the functioning of the brain.

Now, the facts of neurology

> compellingly demonstrate . . . that everything about the mind, from the sensory-motor periphery to the inner sense of self is

minutely controlled by the brain: if your brain lacks certain chemicals or gets locally damaged, your mind is apt to fall apart at the seams. . . . If parts of the mind depend for their existence upon parts of the brain, then the whole of the mind must so depend too. Hence the soul dies with the brain, which is to say it is mortal. [*London Review of Books,* January 23, 1986.]

It should be emphasized that this argument does *not* start from the premise that after a person is dead he never again acts in the world. A correspondent in the *London Review* replied to McGinn by observing that we do not need his or the neuropathologist's "assistance to learn that all behavior stops at death." Similarly, John Stuart Mill in his chapter on "Immortality" in *Three Essays on Religion* thought the argument inconclusive on the ground that the absence of any acts by an individual after his death is as consistent with the view that he will "recommence" his existence "elsewhere" as it is with the assumption that he has been extinguished forever. Such remarks are due to a misunderstanding. The body-mind dependence argument is based on the observed dependence of our mental states and processes and not only our behavior on the body and the brain.

No Distinction Between Soul and Body

I do not think that personal immortality is probable—taking personal immortality to mean continuous individual consciousness, including memory of one's present life on earth. The distinction between soul and body is a verbal one; the reality looks as if it were something psychosomatic, the two aspects being inseparable. So I think it is probable that the psychic part, as far as it is personal psyche, goes the same way as the body.

Arnold Joseph Toynbee in *What Happens When You Die,* 1968.

It should be noted that, if valid, the argument does not merely rule out the survival of human beings as disembodied minds. It equally tells against reincarnation and also against the view that the mind will go on existing in conjunction with a resurrection replica. This is so because it concludes that my mind depends on *my* brain. It does not merely support the less specific conclusion that my mind needs *some* brain as its foundation. If my mind is finished when my brain dies, then it cannot transmigrate to any other body. Similarly, if God created a duplicate of my body containing a duplicate of my brain, *my* mind would not be able to make use of it since it stopped existing with the death of my original body.

Not only reincarnationist believers in survival therefore have a stake in rebutting this argument. I am familiar with a great many such rebuttals, but all the more significant ones can be reduced to two. Before looking at these rejoinders I would like to consider two concrete cases of body-mind dependence. These will help to bring out the full force of the argument. The first is Alzheimer's disease, a dreadful affliction that ruins the last years of a sizable percentage of the world's population. Almost everybody above the age of thirty has known some elderly relative or friend afflicted with this illness. I can therefore be brief in my description of what happens to Alzheimer patients. In the early stages the person misses appointments, he constantly loses and mislays objects, and he frequently cannot recall events in the recent past. As the illness progresses he can no longer read or write and his speech tends to be incoherent. In nursing homes Alzheimer patients commonly watch television, but there is no evidence that they understand what is happening on the screen. The decline in intellectual function is generally accompanied by severe emotional symptoms, such as extreme irritability and violent reactions to persons in the environment, as well as hallucinations and paranoid fears. In the final stages the patient is totally confused, frequently incontinent, and quite unable to recognize anybody, including the closest relatives and friends. At present Alzheimer's is incurable and, unlike in the case of Parkinson's disease, there are no known means of slowing down the deterioration. It is also as yet a mystery why Alzheimer's strikes certain individuals while sparing the majority of old people. However, a great deal is known about what goes on in the brains of Alzheimer patients. Alois Alzheimer, the neurologist after whom the disease is named, found in 1906 that the cerebral cortex and the hippocampus of his patients contained twisted tangles and filaments as well as abnormal neurites known as "neuritic" or "senile plaques." It has since been determined that the density of these abnormal components is directly proportional to the severity of the disorder. Autopsies have shown that Alzheimer victims have a vastly reduced level of an enzyme called "choline acetyltransferase," which is needed for producing the neurotransmitter acetylcholine. Although the reduced level of the enzyme and the neurotransmitter appear in the cortex, the origin of the trouble lies in another region of the brain, the nucleus basalis, which is situated just above the place where the optic nerves meet and cross. Autopsies have revealed a dramatic loss of neurons from the nucleus basalis in Alzheimer victims, and this explains why so little of the enzyme is manufactured in their brains.

Alzheimer's and the Mind

The information just summarized has been culled from articles about Alzheimer's that have appeared in magazines and popular science monthlies in recent years. The authors of these articles are evidently not concerned with the question of survival after death, but they invariably use such phrases as "destruction of the mind" in describing what happens to the victims. In an article in *Science 84* entitled "The Clouded Mind," the author, Michael Shodell, speaks of Alzheimer's as "an illness that destroys the mind, leaving the body behind as a grim reminder of the person who once was there." Similarly, the cover story in *Newsweek* for December 3, 1984, which contained many heart-rending illustrations and listed some of the famous men and women who are suffering from Alzheimer's, was entitled "A Slow Death of the Mind." I think that these descriptions are entirely appropriate: A person who can no longer read or write, whose memory has largely disappeared, whose speech is incoherent, and who is totally indifferent to his environment has in effect lost all or most of what we normally call his mind. The relevance of this to our discussion is obvious. While still alive, an Alzheimer patient's brain is severely damaged and most of his mind has disappeared. After his death his brain is not merely damaged but completely destroyed. It is surely logical to conclude that now his mind is also gone. It seems preposterous to assert that, when the brain is completely destroyed, the mind suddenly returns intact, with its emotional and intellectual capacities, including its memory, restored. How does the *complete* destruction of the brain bring about a cure that has so far totally eluded medical science?

People in Comas

The same obviously applies to people in irreversible comas. Karen Ann Quinlan lay in a coma for over ten years before she finally died. The damage to her brain had made her, in the phrase used by the newspapers, nothing more than a "vegetable." Her E.E.G. was flat; she was unable to speak or write; visits by her foster parents did not register the slightest response. A more recent widely publicized case was that of the great American tenor Jan Peerce. Peerce had amazed the musical public by singing right into his seventies with only a slight decline in his vocal powers. In the end, however, he was felled by two severe strokes, and he spent the last year of his life in an irreversible coma. Relatives and friends could get no response of any kind. Peerce died in December 1984, and Karen Ann Quinlan in June 1985. Did the total destruction of the bodies of these individuals suddenly bring back their emotional and intellectual capacities? If so, where were these during the intervening periods?

The first of the two rejoinders I will consider does not dispute the manifold dependence of mental functions on brain processes. It is claimed, however, that these facts are not inconsistent with

191

survival. They are indeed compatible with the view that the mind is annihilated at death, but they are also compatible with the very different position that the mind continues to exist but has lost its "instrument" for manifesting itself in the world and hence for communicating with people who are still alive. Variants of this argument are found in numerous Protestant theologians of the early decades of the twentieth century, in Catholic writers and also in a number of purely secular philosophers. . . .

The Case of Mrs. D.

I would like to show that the rejoinder . . . is hopelessly inadequate. By retrodictive extrapolation to cases like Alzheimer patients or people in comas one can see that the alternative it proposes to the annihilation theory is absurd. Let us consider the behavior of Alzheimer patients in the later stages of their affliction. The more specific the case, the clearer the implications of the rival views will appear. The mother of a close friend of mine, Mrs. D., recently died from Alzheimer's after suffering from the disease for about eight years. Mrs. D. was a prosperous lady from Virginia, the widow of a banker. In her pre-Alzheimer days she was a courteous and well-behaved person, and she had of course no difficulty recognizing her daughter or any of her other relatives or friends. I do not know what her feelings were about paralyzed people, but my guess is that she pitied them and certainly had no wish to beat them up. As her illness progressed she was put into a nursing home run by nuns who were renowned for their gentle and compassionate ways. She shared a room with an older lady who was paralyzed. For the first year or so Mrs. D. did not become violent. Then she started hitting the nurses. At about the time when she could no longer recognize her daughter, she beat up the paralyzed lady on two or three occasions. From then on she had to be confined to the "seventh floor," which was reserved for violent and exceptionally difficult patients. Let us now see what the survival theorists would have to say about Mrs. D.'s behavior. It should be remembered that on this view Mrs. D., after her death, will exist with her mind intact and will only lack the means of communicating with people on earth. This view implies that throughout her affliction with Alzheimer's Mrs. D.'s mind *was* intact. She recognized her daughter but had lost her ability to express this recognition. She had no wish to beat up an inoffensive paralyzed old woman. On the contrary, "inside" she was the same considerate person as before the onset of the illness. It is simply that her brain disease prevented her from acting in accordance with her true emotions. I must insist that these *are* the implications of the theory that the mind survives the death of the brain and that the brain is only an instrument for communication.

Surely these consequences are absurd: The facts are that Mrs. D. no longer recognized her daughter and that she no longer had any compassionate feelings about paralyzed old women. At any rate, we have the same grounds for saying this as we do in any number of undisputed cases in which people do not suffer from Alzheimer's and fail to recognize other human beings or fail to feel compassion.

The Painlessness of Death

Death, to the secular humanist, is a case of having ceased to be. Having ceased to be is tantamount to having ceased to care, having ceased to hope or to be disappointed, having ceased to fear. Seen in this way, the contemplation of being dead can hardly be more distressing than the contemplation of not yet being conceived, of not yet being conscious. Few there be who suffer over not yet having been before they began to be. Thus, although dying may hurt a lot, though the irrevocable loss of loved ones may hurt excruciatingly, *being* dead does not hurt, even a little.

Delos B. McKown, *Free Inquiry*, Summer 1990.

The guards in Argentine dungeons who tortured and killed liberals had no compassion for their victims, and neither of course did the Nazis who rounded up and then shot Jews in Poland and elsewhere. We have exactly the same kind of evidence for concluding that Mrs. D., who probably did feel compassion for paralyzed people before she suffered from Alzheimer's, no longer felt compassion when beating up her paralyzed roommate. As for memories, all of us sometimes cannot place a familiar tune or remember the name of a person we know well; and in such cases it makes good sense to say that the memories are still there. Even when the name never comes back there is a suspicion that the memory may not have been lost: It is entirely possible that one could bring it back under hypnosis. However, the memory loss in Alzheimer's is totally different, and the same of course applies to people in irreversible comas. It is surely fantastic to maintain that during his last months Jan Peerce did recognize his wife and children and simply could not express his recognition. If anybody makes such a claim it can only be for ulterior metaphysical reasons and not because it is supported by the slightest evidence.

The second rejoinder is . . . sometimes confusingly amalgamated with the first rejoinder, but it is a distinct argument and should be evaluated on its own. It involves a distinction between the mind, which is identical with the phenomenal or empirical self, and another nonphysical entity to which various labels have been applied. . . . It is argued that, although the mind may indeed so closely depend on the body that it must cease with the body's death, the same is not true of the soul. The soul is the "I" that "owns" both the body and the mind. I am five feet seven inches tall, I weigh one hundred and fifty pounds, I have blue eyes and brown hair; but I also have certain sensations and feelings and thoughts. I have various physical skills, and I also possess certain emotional and intellectual dispositions. It is this underlying "I"—the subject of both the body and the mind—that has not been shown to require a body for its existence.

The Soul Is Dependent on the Body

There are two objections to this rejoinder, each of them fatal. In the first place, although the way we speak in certain contexts suggests an underlying subject of both body and mind, there is no reason to suppose that it exists. Hume's theory that human minds are nothing but "bundles of impressions and ideas" is seriously inadequate. Each of us, at least while he is sane, has a sense of his self, more specifically, a sense of himself as continuing the same person from moment to moment. However, what this consists in is not the totally unchanging and metaphysical entity that Hume rightly rebelled against. It is a sense of continuity in certain bodily sensations (especially of our limbs and certain muscle groups) and of our various tastes, opinions, and habits—more generally of our emotional and intellectual dispositions. These, together with our bodies, make us the kinds of persons we are. Although our emotional and intellectual dispositions are subject to change, they are, unlike our moods and sensations, relatively stable. If this is what is meant by "soul," there is no reason to deny that we have a soul; but the soul in this sense is just as dependent on the body and the brain as any particular sensations, feelings, and thoughts. . . .

If there were such a thing as a metaphysical soul, it would not be what anybody means by "I." The great seventeenth-century philosopher Pierre Gassendi, who was both a Catholic priest and an atomistic materialist, professed to believe in such a soul. He also believed that insanity was a brain disease. Since the soul or reason (Gassendi preferred the later word) did not depend on the body, he concluded quite consistently that the soul or reason remained sane even when the individual had become insane. Gassendi's consistency led to a *reductio ad absurdum* of his position. If I go mad and if at the same time my soul remains sane then my soul is not me.

"People frequently ask me if I believe NDEs are evidence of life after life. My answer is yes."

Near-Death Experiences Demonstrate the Existence of an Afterlife

Raymond A. Moody Jr.

Raymond A. Moody Jr., a psychiatrist and author, rose to prominence in 1975 with the publication of *Life After Life*, a study of people who were on the brink of dying, were revived, and reported mystical experiences. In the following viewpoint, he describes the common features of what he calls the near-death experience (NDE), and rebuts arguments that they are mere hallucinations. Moody concludes that these experiences provide evidence for life after death.

As you read, consider the following questions:

1. What are the stages of a typical near-death experience, according to Moody?
2. How are people affected by the near-death experience, according to the author?
3. Why does Moody reject the theory that NDEs are simply memories of birth?

We are no closer to answering the basic question of the afterlife now than we were thousands of years ago when it was first pondered by the ancients. But there are many ordinary people who have been to the brink of death and reported miraculous glimpses of a world beyond, a world that glows with love and understanding, that can be reached only by an exciting trip through a tunnel or passageway. . . .

In my first book, *Life After Life*, I posed many questions I couldn't answer and raised the ire of skeptics who found the case studies of a few hundred people to be worthless in the realm of "real" scientific study. Many doctors claimed that they had never heard of the near-death experience (NDE), despite having resuscitated hundreds of people.

Others claimed it was simply a form of mental illness, like schizophrenia. Some said these NDEs happened only to extremely religious people, while others felt they were a form of demon possession. These experiences never happen to children, some doctors said, because they haven't been "culturally polluted" like adults. Too few people have NDEs for the experience to be significant, others said.

Some people were interested in researching the subject of NDEs further, myself included. The work we have done has shed a tremendous amount of light on this subject. We have been able to address most of the questions put forth by those who feel that the near-death experience is little more than a mental illness or the brain playing tricks on itself.

A Sense of Being Dead

Many people don't realize that their near-death experiences have anything to do with death. They find themselves floating above their body, looking at it from a distance, and suddenly feel fear and/or confusion. They wonder, "How can I be up here, looking at myself down there?" At this point, they may not actually recognize the physical body they are looking at as their own. . . .

Out-of-Body-Experience (OBE). About the time that the doctor says "We've lost him," the patient undergoes a complete change of perspective. He feels himself rising up and viewing his own body below.

Most people say they are not just some spot of consciousness when this happens. They still seem to have a kind of body even though they are out of their physical bodies. They say this spiritual body has shape and form unlike that of our physical bodies. Although most are at a loss to explain what it looks like, some describe it as a cloud of colors, or an energy field. . . .

The Tunnel Experience. The tunnel experience generally happens after bodily separation. I didn't notice until I wrote *Life*

After Life that it isn't until people undergo the "cutting of ribbons" and the out-of-body experience that they realize that their experience has something to do with death.

A Being of Light

The most common phenomenon in Western reports of the near-death experience (NDE) is the experience of passing through a tunnel and then seeing a brilliant light, or meeting a great being of light—a being that has incredible wisdom and intelligence and bliss. The particular individual's religious belief does not matter here; atheists have this experience as often as true believers. This fact, in itself, tends to corroborate the idea that, in the dying process, one does contact some of the subtler dimensions of existence.

Ken Wilber in *What Survives?*, 1990.

At this point, a portal or tunnel opens to them and they are propelled into darkness. They start going through this dark space, and at the end they come into the brilliant light. . . .

The tunnel experience is not something I discovered. A fifteenth-century painting by Hieronymous Bosch called "The Ascent into the Empyrean" visually describes this experience. In the foreground people are dying, surrounded by spiritual beings who are trying to direct their attention upward. They pass through a dark tunnel and come out into a light. As they go into this light, they kneel reverently.

One tunnel experience was described to me as being almost infinite in length and width and filled with light. The descriptions are many, but the sense of what is happening remains the same: The person is going through a passageway toward an intense light.

People of Light. Once through the tunnel, the person usually meets beings of light. Not composed of ordinary light, these beings glow with a beautiful and intense luminescence that seems to permeate everything, filling the viewer with love. In fact, one person who went through this experience said, "I could describe this as 'light' or 'love' and it would mean the same thing." Some say it's almost like being drenched by a rainstorm of light. . . .

In this situation, NDEers frequently meet up with deceased friends and relatives. These people often appear in the same indescribable bodies as the NDEers'.

Besides bright light and luminescent friends and relatives, some people have described beautiful pastoral scenes. One woman I know spoke of a meadow that was surrounded by plants, each with its own inner light. Occasionally, people see beautiful cities of light that defy description in their grandeur. . . .

The Being of Light. After meeting several beings of light, the NDEer usually meets a supreme being of light. People with a Christian background often describe it as God or Jesus. Those of other religious traditions may call it Buddha or Allah. Still others have said that it's neither God nor Jesus, but someone very holy nonetheless.

Love and Understanding

Whoever it is, the being radiates love and understanding—so much so, that most people want to be with it forever.

But they can't. At this point they are told, usually by the being of light, that they have to return to their earthly body. But the being will first take them on a review of their lives.

The Life Review. When the life review occurs, there are no physical surroundings. In their place is a full-color, three-dimensional, panoramic review of everything the NDEer has ever done. . . .

Through all of this, the being of light is with them, asking what good they have done with their lives. The being helps them through this review, putting the events of their lives in perspective.

Everyone who goes through this comes away believing that the most important thing in life is love.

For most, the second most important thing in life is knowledge. When people come back they have a thirst for knowledge.

Reluctance to Return. For many, the NDE is such a pleasant event that they don't want to return, and they are frequently very angry at their doctors for bringing them back. . . .

NDEers may behave this way, but it is a short-lived feeling. A week or so afterward, they are happy to have returned. Although they miss the blissful state, they are glad to have the chance to go on living. . . .

Personal Transformations

There is one common element in all near-death experiences: They transform the people who have them. In twenty years of studying NDEers, I have never talked to one who hasn't undergone a very deep and positive transformation as a result of the experience.

I don't mean to imply that an NDE turns individuals into syrupy, uncritical Pollyannas. Although it certainly makes them more positive and pleasant to be around (especially if they weren't too pleasant before the near-death experience), it also leads to an active engagement with the world. It helps them grapple with unpleasant aspects of reality in an unemotional and clear-thinking way—a way that is new to them. . . .

"Have you learned to love?" is a question almost all NDEers face during their experience. Upon returning, they say that love is the most important thing in life. Many say it is why we are here. Most find it the hallmark of happiness and fulfillment, with other values paling beside it. . . .

Attempts to Explain NDEs

There are many attempts to explain near-death experiences as something other than spiritual events or glimpses into the other-world. . . .

Carl Sagan, Ph.D., noted Cornell University astronomer, is among those who have tried to explain the tunnel experience as a left-over memory from the experience of birth. That everyone experiences birth could explain why NDEs are similar, whether they occur in a Buddhist or a Baptist culture. Struggling down the birth canal and being pulled into a bright and colorful world by people who are glad to see you are things most of us have experienced.

It is no wonder that Sagan makes the connection between birth and death. In his best-selling book, *Broca's Brain: Reflections on the Romance of Science*, Sagan writes: "The only alternative, so far as I can see, is that every human being, without exception, has already shared an experience like that of those travelers who return from the land of death: the sensation of flight; the emergence from darkness into light; an experience in which, at least sometimes, a heroic figure can be dimly perceived, bathed in radiance and glory. There is only one common experience that matches this description. It is called birth." Carl Becker, Ph.D., philosophy professor at the University of Hawaii at Manoa, examined pediatric research to determine just how much a child knows at birth and can remember of the experience. His conclusion: Babies don't remember being born and don't have the faculties to retain the experience in the brain.

Becker argues that infant perception is too poor to see what is going on during birth. . . .

Another point supported by studies is that children have little memory for shapes or patterns. And since their brains are not well developed and have not yet been exposed to life outside the womb, they have little capacity for encoding what they see.

One final note on Sagan's theory: The tunnel experience most often involves a rapid passage toward a light at the end of the tunnel. In the actual birth experience, a child's face is pressed against the walls of the birth canal. Infants are not looking up at an approaching light, as Sagan's theory suggests. They can see nothing as they are pushed toward their entrance into the world.

The tunnel experience has been called by some "the gateway into the other world," and is generally described as the feeling one would have speeding through a tunnel toward an ever-growing dot of light at the end.

Some researchers feel that the tunnel experience is caused by the brain's reaction to increased levels of carbon dioxide (CO_2) in the blood. This gas is a by-product of the body's metabolism—oxygen is breathed in and air containing higher levels of CO_2 is breathed out. When a person stops breathing because of a heart attack or severe trauma, the bloodstream's CO_2 level rises rapidly. When the level gets too high, tissues begin to die.

Because CO_2 inhalation was used in the '50s as a form of psychotherapy, it has been experienced by a number of patients and its symptoms are well known. Case studies of this no-longer-used therapy describe the experience as feeling like a trip down a tunnel or cone, or being surrounded by bright lights.

It hasn't been reported that CO_2 inhalation is accompanied by such things as beings of light and life reviews.

I could almost accept the belief that too much CO_2 causes the tunnel experience if not for the research of Michael Sabom, M.D., an Atlanta cardiologist.

In one of his cases, Sabom coincidentally measured the blood oxygen levels of a patient at the very moment of his NDE and found the patient's oxygen level to be above normal. If anything, Sabom's case study shows the need for further research.

Must NDEers Be Near Death?

Many skeptics contend that NDEs are caused by stress or illness on the body. Although they admit that NDEs happen to people who nearly die, they also think the same experience happens to those who are seriously—but not critically—ill.

To test this theory, Melvin Morse, M.D., a Seattle pediatrician, interviewed eleven children aged three through sixteen who had survived brushes with death. They included cardiac arrest victims and youngsters who had been in comas. Seven of these children had elements of the near-death experience, including memories of being out of their bodies, entering darkness, being in a tunnel, and deciding to return to their bodies.

These eleven patients were compared with twenty-nine children the same age who had survived serious illnesses that didn't involve brushes with death. None of this group had memories of any elements of the NDE.

Morse and his fellow researchers concluded that "regardless of the . . . cause of these unique experiences, it is clear that children who survive life-threatening events [have] NDEs." Thus the near-death experience is something that is specifically connected with being on the brink of death as opposed to just being sick.

Some people postulate that NDEs are merely hallucinations, mental events brought on by stress, lack of oxygen, or in some cases even drugs. However, one of the strongest arguments against the NDE-as-hallucination is its occurrence in patients whose electroencephalogram (EEG) readings are absolutely flat.

The EEG measures the brain's electrical activity, recording it by inscribing a line on a continuous strip of paper. This line goes up and down in response to the brain's electrical activity when a person thinks, speaks, dreams, or does virtually anything. If the brain is dead, the EEG reading is a flat line, which implies that the brain is incapable of thought or action. A flat EEG is now the legal definition of death in many states.

Eight Million People

A Gallup Poll indicated more than 8 million Americans report having undergone an NDE. How many outside of the United States put forth the same claim is unknown, but it is surely safe to assume that the number is huge.

Vernon Pizer, *American Legion Magazine*, August 1991.

But there are many cases in which people with flat EEGs have had near-death experiences. They, of course, lived to tell about them. The sheer number of these people indicates that at least with some people, the NDEs have occurred when they were technically dead. Had these been hallucinations, they would have shown up on the EEG.

I should say that EEGs are not always an exact measure of brain life. Sometimes, the brain can be alive at such a low level that the EEG doesn't register the activity. . . .

A Way to Cope with Death

Some believe that NDEs are the mind's mechanism for coping with our worst reality—death. Accordingly, the grimness of the situation leads the mind to trick itself into a better situation. . . .

Those unable to face their rapidly approaching death may deny it by creating a fantasy that they survive. This is a form of wish fulfillment. It's defensive in nature because it pretends to defend us from final annihilation.

The most obvious argument against it is that all NDEers have basically the same experience. Were it merely wish fulfillment, the NDE reports would be entirely different, with no common bonds.

Another difficulty with this explanation is that a psychological defense like wish fulfillment maintains your status quo, since the psyche wants to be kept intact. A near-death experience is quite different in that it represents a breakthrough. Instead of keeping people as they are, it makes them face their lives in a way that they have never done before.

After NDEs, people face personal truth in a profound way. And it makes them happy. Unlike the wish fulfillment known as daydreaming, which provides temporary relief from the world around us, the NDE is a platform for lifelong change.

For more than twenty years, I have worked on the cutting edge of NDE research. In the course of my studies, I have listened to thousands of people tell about their deeply personal journeys into . . . what? The world beyond? The heaven they learned about from their religion? A region of the brain that reveals itself only in times of desperation?

I have talked to almost every NDE researcher in the world about his or her work. Most of us believe in our hearts that NDEs are a glimpse of life after life. But as scientists and people of medicine, we still haven't come up with "scientific proof" that a part of us goes on living after our physical being is dead. Meanwhile, we keep trying to answer in a scientific way that perplexing question: What happens when we die?

I don't think science can ever answer that question. It can be pondered from almost every side, but the answer will never be complete. Even if the near-death experience were duplicated in a laboratory setting, then what? Science would only hear more about a journey that can't be verified.

Evidence for the Afterlife

People frequently ask me if I believe NDEs are evidence of life after life. My answer is yes.

There are several things that make me feel so strongly. One is the out-of-body experiences in which NDEers report details about the attempts to save their lives. The most impressive thing to me about NDEs is the enormous changes in personality they bring about in people. That NDEs totally transform those who experience them demonstrates their reality and power. Based on such examinations, I am convinced that NDEers do get a glimpse of the beyond, a brief passage into a whole other reality.

"NDEs [near-death experiences] provide no evidence for life after death."

Near-Death Experiences Do Not Demonstrate the Existence of an Afterlife

Susan Blackmore

Thousands of people have reported near-death experiences (NDEs), and some people have argued that such accounts provide evidence for an afterlife. In the following viewpoint, Susan Blackmore disputes this view and provides an alternate explanation for such experiences. She argues that NDEs result from memories and reactions within the brain. Blackmore is a psychologist at the Brain Perception Laboratory at the University of Bristol in Great Britain.

As you read, consider the following questions:

1. What does Blackmore find inadequate about the theory that NDEs are just hallucinations?
2. How might brain structure explain NDEs, according to the author?
3. Why does Blackmore argue that NDEs change lives?

Susan Blackmore, "Near-Death Experiences: In or Out of the Body?" *Skeptical Inquirer*, Fall 1991. Reprinted with permission.

What is it like to die? Although most of us fear death to a greater or lesser extent, there are now more and more people who have "come back" from states close to death and have told stories of usually very pleasant and even joyful experiences at death's door.

For many experiencers, their adventures seem unquestionably to provide evidence for life after death, and the profound effects the experience can have on them is just added confirmation. By contrast, for many scientists these experiences are just hallucinations produced by the dying brain and of no more interest than an especially vivid dream.

So which is right? Are near-death experiences (NDEs) the prelude to our life after death or the very last experience we have before oblivion? I shall argue that neither is quite right: NDEs provide no evidence for life after death, and we can best understand them by looking at neurochemistry, physiology, and psychology; but they are much more interesting than any dream. They seem completely real and can transform people's lives. Any satisfactory theory has to understand that too—and that leads us to questions about minds, selves, and the nature of consciousness. . . .

Near-Death Experiences

Resuscitation from ever more serious heart failure has provided accounts of extraordinary experiences (although this is not the only cause of NDEs). These remained largely ignored until about 15 years ago, when Raymond Moody (1975), an American physician, published his best-selling *Life After Life*. He had talked with many people who had "come back from death," and he put together an account of a typical NDE. In this idealized experience a person hears himself pronounced dead. Then comes a loud buzzing or ringing noise and a long, dark tunnel. He can see his own body from a distance and watch what is happening. Soon he meets others and a "being of light" who shows him a playback of events from his life and helps him to evaluate it. At some point he gets to a barrier and knows that he has to go back. Even though he feels joy, love, and peace there, he returns to his body and life. Later he tries to tell others; but they don't understand, and he soon gives up. Nevertheless the experience deeply affects him, especially his views about life and death. . . .

Perhaps we should . . . conclude that all the experiences are "just imagination" or "nothing but hallucinations." However, this is the weakest theory of all. The experiences must, in some sense, be hallucinations, but this is not, on its own, any explanation. We have to ask why are they these kinds of hallucinations? Why tunnels?

Some say the tunnel is a symbolic representation of the gateway to another world. But then why always a tunnel and not, say, a gate, doorway, or even the great River Styx? Why the light at the end of the tunnel? and why always above the body, not below it? I have no objection to the theory that the experiences are hallucinations. I only object to the idea that you can explain them by saying, "They are just hallucinations." This explains nothing. A viable theory would answer these questions without dismissing the experiences. That, even if only in tentative form, is what I shall try to provide.

The Physiology of the Tunnel: Tunnels do not only occur near death. They are also experienced in epilepsy and migraine, when falling asleep, meditating, or just relaxing, with pressure on both eyeballs, and with certain drugs, such as LSD, psilocybin, and mescaline. I have experienced them many times myself. It is as though the whole world becomes a rushing, roaring tunnel and you are flying along it toward a bright light at the end. No doubt many readers have also been there, for surveys show that about a third of people have. . . .

In the 1930s, Heinrich Kluver, at the University of Chicago, noted four form constants in hallucinations: the tunnel, the spiral, the lattice or grating, and the cobweb. Their origin probably lies in the structure of the visual cortex, the part of the brain that processes visual information. Imagine that the outside world is mapped onto the back of the eye (on the retina), and then again in the cortex. The mathematics of this mapping (at least to a reasonable approximation) is well known.

Mapping the Brain

Jack Cowan, a neurobiologist at the University of Chicago, has used this mapping to account for the tunnel. Brain activity is normally kept stable by some cells inhibiting others. Disinhibition (the reduction of this inhibitory activity) produces too much activity in the brain. This can occur near death (because of lack of oxygen) or with drugs like LSD, which interfere with inhibition. Cowan uses an analogy with fluid mechanics to argue that disinhibition will induce stripes of activity that move across the cortex. Using the mapping it can easily be shown that stripes in the cortex would appear like concentric rings or spirals in the visual world. In other words, if you have stripes in the cortex you will seem to see a tunnel-like pattern of spirals or rings.

This theory is important in showing how the structure of the brain could produce the same hallucination for everyone. However, I was dubious about the idea of these moving stripes, and also Cowan's theory doesn't readily explain the bright light at the center. So Tom Troscianko and I, at the University of Bristol, tried to develop a simpler theory. The most obvious thing about the representation in the cortex is that there are lots of cells representing the center of the visual field but very few for the edges. This means that you can see small things very clearly in the center, but if they are out at the edges you cannot. We took just this simple fact as a starting point and used a computer to simulate what would happen when you have gradually increasing electrical noise in the visual cortex.

The computer program starts with thinly spread dots of light, mapped in the same way as the cortex, with more toward the middle and very few at the edges. Gradually the number of dots increases, mimicking the increasing noise. Now the center begins to look like a white blob and the outer edges gradually get more and more dots. And so it expands until eventually the whole screen is filled with light. The appearance is just like a dark speckly tunnel with a white light at the end, and the light grows bigger and bigger (or nearer and nearer) until it fills the whole screen. . . .

According to this kind of theory there is, of course, no real tunnel. Nevertheless there is a real physical cause of the tunnel experience. It is noise in the visual cortex. This way we can explain the origin of the tunnel without just dismissing the experiences and without needing to invent other bodies or other worlds.

Out of the Body Experiences: Like tunnels, OBEs are not confined to near death. They too can occur when just relaxing and falling asleep, with meditation, and in epilepsy and migraine. They can also, at least by a few people, be induced at will. I have been interested in OBEs since I had a long and dramatic experience myself.

It is important to remember that these experiences seem quite real. People don't describe them as dreams or fantasies but as events that actually happened. This is, I presume, why they seek explanations in terms of other bodies or other worlds. . . .

What we need is a theory that involves no unmeasurable entities or untestable other worlds but explains why the experiences happen and why they seem so real.

What Is Real?

I would start by asking why anything seems real. You might think this is obvious—after all, the things we see out there are real, aren't they? Well no, in a sense they aren't. As perceiving creatures all we know is what our senses tell us. And our senses tell us what is "out there" by constructing models of the world with ourselves in it. The whole of the world "out there" and our own bodies are really constructions of our minds. Yet we are sure, all the time, that this construction—if you like, this "model of reality"—is "real" while the other fleeting thoughts we have are unreal. We call the rest of them daydreams, imagination, fantasies, and so on. Our brains have no trouble distinguishing "reality" from "imagination." But this distinction is not given. It is one the brain has to make for itself by deciding which of its own models represents the world "out there." I suggest it does this by comparing all the models it has at any time and choosing the most stable one as "reality."

This will normally work very well. The model created by the senses is the best and most stable the system has. It is obviously "reality," while that image I have of the bar I'm going to go to later is unstable and brief. The choice is easy. By comparison, when you are almost asleep, very frightened, or nearly dying, the model from the senses will be confused and unstable. If you are under terrible stress or suffering oxygen deprivation, then the choice won't be so easy. All the models will be unstable.

So what will happen now? Possibly the tunnel being created by noise in the visual cortex will be the most stable model and so, according to my supposition, this will seem real. Fantasies and imagery might become more stable than the sensory model, and so seem real. The system will have lost input control.

What then should a sensible biological system do to get back to normal? I would suggest that it could try to ask itself—as it were—"Where am I? What is happening?" Even a person under severe stress will have some memory left. They might recall the accident, or know that they were in hospital for an operation, or remember the pain of the heart attack. So they will try to reconstruct, from what little they can remember, what is happening.

Now we know something very interesting about memory models. Often they are constructed in a bird's-eye view. That is, the events or scenes are seen as though from above. If you find this strange, try to remember the last time you went to a pub or the last time you walked along the seashore. Where are "you" looking from in this recalled scene? If you are looking from above you will see what I mean.

So my explanation of the OBE becomes clear. A memory model in bird's-eye view has taken over from the sensory model. It seems perfectly real because it is the best model the system has got at the time. Indeed, it seems real for just the same reason anything ever seems real.

Testable Predictions

This theory of the OBE leads to many testable predictions, for example, that people who habitually use bird's-eye views should be more likely to have OBEs. Both Harvey Irwin (1986), an Australian psychologist, and myself have found that people who dream as though they were spectators have more OBEs, although there seems to be no difference for the waking use of different viewpoints. I have also found that people who can more easily switch viewpoints in their imagination are also more likely to report OBEs. . . .

The Life Review: The experience of seeing excerpts from your life flash before you is not really as mysterious as it first seems. It has long been known that stimulation of cells in the temporal lobe of the brain can produce instant experiences that seem like the reliving of memories. Also, temporal-lobe epilepsy can produce similar experiences, and such seizures can involve other limbic structures in the brain, such as the amygdala and hippocampus, which are also associated with memory.

Imagine that the noise in the dying brain stimulates cells like this. The memories will be aroused and, according to my hypothesis, if they are the most stable model the system has at that time they will seem real. For the dying person they may well be more stable than the confused and noisy sensory model.

The link between temporal-lobe epilepsy and the NDE has formed the basis of a thorough neurobiological model of the NDE, [which] suggests that the brain stress consequent on the near-death episode leads to the release of neuropeptides and neurotransmitters (in particular the endogenous endorphins). These then stimulate the limbic system and other connected areas. In addition, the effect of the endorphins could account for the blissful and other positive emotional states so often associated with the NDE. . . .

Of course there is more to the life review than just memories. The person feels as though she or he is judging these life events, being shown their significance and meaning. But this too, I suggest, is not so very strange. When the normal world of the senses is gone and memories seem real, our perspective on our life changes. We can no longer be so attached to our plans, hopes, ambitions, and fears, which fade away and become unimportant, while the past comes to life again. We can only accept it as it is, and there is no one to judge it but ourselves. This is, I think, why so many NDEers say they faced their past life with acceptance and equanimity.

NDEs Describe Dying, Not Death

There are some fundamental problems with the notion that survivors have actually experienced death—and what lies beyond. There is a basic confusion about the definition of death, which in recent years has been revised to mean complete brain death. What NDEs reflect, then, is not death but the dying process. No reliable evidence exists to show that people who report such experiences have died and returned, which would seem to be required for a glimpse of the hereafter. Nor is there any evidence that consciousness exists separately from the brain or body. What these people have experienced is an altered state of consciousness presumably associated with the changes taking place in a dying brain.

Paul Kurtz, *Psychology Today*, September 1988.

Other World: Now we come to what might seem the most extraordinary parts of the NDE; the worlds beyond the tunnel and OBE. But I think you can now see that they are not so extraordinary at all. In this state the outside world is no longer real, and inner worlds are. Whatever we can imagine clearly enough will seem real. And what will we imagine when we know we are dying? I am sure for many people it is the world they expect or hope to see. Their minds may turn to people they have known who have died before them or to the world they hope to enter next. Like the other images we have been considering, these will seem perfectly real.

Finally, there are those aspects of the NDE that are ineffable—they cannot be put into words. I suspect that this is because some people take yet another step, a step into nonbeing. I shall try to explain this by asking another question. What is consciousness? If you say it is a thing, another body, a substance, you will only get into the kinds of difficulty we got into with OBEs. I prefer to say that consciousness is just what it is like being a mental model. In other words, all the mental models in any person's mind are all conscious, but only one is a model of "me." This is the one that I think of as myself and to which I relate everything else. It gives a core to my life. It allows me to think that I am a person, something that lives on all the time. It allows me to ignore the fact that "I" change from moment to moment and even disappear every night in sleep.

Now when the brain comes close to death, this model of self may simply fall apart. Now there is no self. It is a strange and dramatic experience. For there is no longer an experiencer—yet there is experience.

This state is obviously hard to describe, for the "you" who is trying to describe it cannot imagine not being. Yet this profound experience leaves its mark. The self never seems quite the same again.

The After Effects: I think we can now see why an essentially physiological event can change people's lives so profoundly. The experience has jolted their usual (and erroneous) view of the relationship between themselves and the world. We all too easily assume that we are some kind of persistent entity inhabiting a perishable body. But, as the Buddha taught we have to see through that illusion. The world is only a construction of an information-processing system, and the self is too. I believe that the NDE gives people a glimpse into the nature of their own minds that is hard to get any other way. Drugs can produce it temporarily, mystical experiences can do it for rare people, and long years of practice in meditation or mindfulness can do it. But the NDE can out of the blue strike anyone and show them what they never knew before, that their body is only that—a lump of flesh—that they are not so very important after all. And that is a very freeing and enlightening experience.

No More Self

If my analysis of the NDE is correct, we can extrapolate to the next stage. Lack of oxygen first produces increased activity through disinhibition, but eventually it all stops. Since it is this activity that produces the mental models that give rise to consciousness, then all this will cease. There will be no more experience, no more self, and so that, as far as my constructed self is concerned, is the end.

So, are NDEs in or out of the body? I should say neither, for neither experiences nor selves have any location. It is finally death that dissolves the illusion that we are a solid self inside a body.

"Death, for all its mystery and starkness and seeming darkness, leads, for the believer, to something better than life."

A Belief in an Afterlife Gives Life Meaning

Timothy K. Jones

Whether or not one believes in life after death can have a profound impact on how one approaches life and death. Writing from a Christian perspective, Timothy K. Jones in the following viewpoint argues that the present life is a mere prelude to what happens after death. He states that such an outlook on death can give one's life special significance. Jones is an associate features editor at *Christianity Today*, an evangelical magazine.

As you read, consider the following questions:

1. Why are Americans preoccupied with health and fitness, according to Jones?
2. How has the author's approach toward daily living been affected by his beliefs in an afterlife?
3. What does Jones mean when he states that the meaning of life is found beyond life?

Timothy K. Jones, "Death in the Mirror," *Christianity Today*, June 24, 1991. Copyright 1991, Christianity Today. Reprinted with permission.

One Friday night some months ago, I stood by my bedroom window and listened to my apartment neighbor downstairs bellow threats to kill me. I suppose the sound of my boys' feet on their floor above his room set off his drunken rage. I had never experienced a threat on my life; his curses and explosion of anger left me shaking. The fear subsided slowly, even after police arrived to calm him.

Life's Transience

But the encounter was not my only recent brush with mortality. Some months earlier I was lying in bed, drowsily waiting for sleep, when I was jarred awake by the thought that this year of my life, my thirty-fifth, is one of an ever-depleting supply. In the shadows of a winter night I had a glimpse of the transience of life—*my* life.

It was like the experience of Antonio Parr in Frederick Buechner's *Open Heart*. As he stood at the Brooklyn graveside of his twin sister, "some stirring of the air or quick movement of squirrel or bird brought me back to myself," Parr recounts, "and just at that instant . . . I knew that the self I'd been brought back to was some fine day going to be as dead as Miriam. . . . Through grace alone I banged right into it—not a lesson this time, a collision."

Antonio and I are not alone. "All of a sudden," writes Michael Specter in the *New Republic*, "a generation taught first to trust nobody over 30, and then to seek fulfillment through accumulated goods, has stumbled over the notion of its eventual demise." Children of the "now" moment are being brought to the brink of a larger truth, a longer frame of reference.

But how are they dealing with the haunting discovery that life, as the psalmist wrote, is but a few handbreadths? Successful young people, Specter notes, are "hustling for the 'right' cemetery spot in much the same way they have scoured the nation for the most sophisticated cabernets, the most authentic Italian espresso machines, and the best Aprica strollers." They are scrambling for a peace of mind they hope can be theirs for the price of a prestigious grave site. Though some people are concerned about death's reality, they are not also moved to search out death's *meaning* or ponder its ultimate outcome.

But that is precisely what my nighttime encounters have set in motion in me. Intimations of the transience of this life make me wonder more about the everlasting dimensions of the *next* life. I am thinking about heaven, feeling more the eternal weight of glory, and it is changing how I live.

Such talk, of course, seems awkward, if not odd, in today's society, where youthful vigor provides the implicit model for a fulfilling life. This is surely related to our culture's focus on (sometimes obsession with) the present. "There is no cure," said philosopher George Santayana, "for birth and death save to enjoy the interval." We prepare best for death, some argue, by not preparing at all—by simply "enjoying the interval." Nor should we cloud the events of today with the eventualities of tomorrow.

Death Is Not Final

Yes, we need a renewed awareness of death. But we need far more. We need a faith, in the midst of our groanings, that death is not the last word, but the next to last. What is mortal will be swallowed up by life. One day all whispers of death will fall silent.

Philip Yancey, *Christianity Today*, May 13, 1988.

Americans, with hospitals and funeral homes to shield them from death's inevitable presence, find it easy to drink deeply from this philosophical stream. That explains, perhaps, our preoccupation with health, our penchant for Nautilus rooms and fad diets. Health, that glorious state of freedom from aching joints and clogging arteries, allows us to forget, for the moment, that our bodies are not indestructible, that a day of physical reckoning awaits.

As one who jogs regularly in the hope of avoiding the heart disease that took my father's life, I am all for conscientious care of the human body. But the thud and pant and grunt of our workouts takes on a zeal that has roots in something else: our desperate eagerness to cheat death and ignore mortality. Interestingly, polled Americans repeatedly list health at the top of their preoccupations—above love, work, money, or anything else. They see it as their primary source of happiness. Why? Perhaps because health helps us forget the finality of our frailty.

Society's obsession with the feel-good satisfactions of the moment explains much else: the pervasive "culture of entertainment," for example, that fills our living rooms and crowds out time to think about growing old. What is even more perplexing is the extent to which Christians join the paean of praise to the present. Even in evangelical churches, I sometimes get the impression that Christianity is mostly about helping people become well-adjusted, happily acclimated residents of the present tense. Rarely have I been reminded of a truth of great comfort to earlier generations of believers: that life here is a training ground for life to come. We may hear, occasionally, a sermon on living as "strangers" and sojourners, which the New Testament enjoins. But we have lost the Puritans' great sense, as J.I. Packer states, that we should "regard readiness to die as the first step in learning to live."

Christian faith, however, has always argued that meaning in life will be found *beyond* life. "In my end is my beginning," the poet T.S. Eliot wrote. Those words are found not only in his early poem "Burnt Norton," but also on his tombstone. In a profound way, where we are headed affects how we travel. And death, for all its mystery and starkness and seeming darkness, leads, for the believer, to something better than life. Despite the richness of this world, the New Testament reminds us that we are on our way to a reality even clearer and more substantial than we presently experience. "Here we do not have an enduring city," the writer to the Hebrews wrote, "but we are looking for the city to come" (Heb. 13:14, NIV). Or, as Paul put it, "We look not to the things that are seen, but to the things that are unseen" (2 Cor. 4:16, 18).

Indeed, we will never live fully if we think we can exhaust the meaning of the moment without reference to the longer stretch. Writer Annie Dillard discovered a related truth while finishing a book at a friend's cabin on northern Puget Sound in Washington. She had to heat the cabin with a kerosene heater and a wood stove. But she did not know how to split wood. "What I did was less like splitting wood than chipping flints. . . . One night . . . I had a dream in which I was given to understand, by the powers that be, how to split wood. You aim, said the dream—of course!—at the chopping block. It is true. You aim at the chopping block, not at the wood; then you split the wood, instead of chipping it. You cannot do the job cleanly unless you treat the wood as the transparent means to an end, by aiming past it."

What is true about writing or splitting pine logs is true about carrying on our lives: We cannot live rightly until we aim *past* life. Eternity provides the only goal that makes ultimate sense of each moment. Seventeenth-century Anglican churchman Jeremy Taylor said it differently: "Since we stay not here, being people but of a day's abode, and our age is like that of a fly and contemporary with a gourd, we must look somewhere else, for an abiding city, a place in another country to fix our house in, whose walls and foundation is God, where we must find rest, or else be restless for ever."

An Awareness of Death

Awareness of death, and of its opening to a life beyond, has not only framed how I look at life. It has also begun to work a change in how I walk through life. It has, in other words, brought not just new meaning to my moments, but changes to my behavior. As Samuel Johnson reportedly said, "When a man knows he is going to be hanged in a fortnight, it concentrates his mind wonderfully." Our awareness of the transitoriness of this life, I find, concentrates my priorities, helps me refashion my daily choices.

To know that life is not a destinationless journey helps me live more completely for a final good, an ultimate end. Says England's bishop of Salisbury, John Baker, "We should think about our death far more, because . . . it makes you say, 'What are the really important things I should be doing with my life, not just selfishly, but for other people? Are there quarrels I'd like to heal, relationships I should mend, something I'd like to do for somebody I keep putting off?'"

But it is more than simply thinking about death that will do it. The Puritan divine Richard Baxter spoke of the attracting, transforming power of what he called the "saints' everlasting rest." In his book by that title, he noted, "As everything inclines to its proper centre, so the rational creature is carried on in all its motion, which desires after its end [our 'everlasting rest']." To know that "we have such a hope," as Paul says, makes us "very bold" (2 Cor. 3:12, NIV). God's gracious assurance and promise of eternal care helps us "incline to our proper centre." Our daily decisions become oriented around something more profound.

Eternal Significance

I am still human enough, of course, that death often seems intimidating. However my shaking encounter with my neighbor might have been a tonic for my soul, it was still harrowing. But a conviction about what lies beyond is giving me courage to live more fully and more faithfully. And I find that thinking about death—even *my* death—is no hangdog, maudlin exercise. Indeed, because of my knowledge of a life to come (which glories I have surely only begun to fathom), the awareness sometimes even brings a sense of certainty and expectation. That helps me realize that whatever happens, however long or short I live, God can take even my frailty and mortality and invest it with eternal significance, and plant within me an unceasing delight.

"All hope that death is not real and all hope for the afterlife is vain, immoral, perverse, and pathological."

Belief in an Afterlife Is Folly

Verle Muhrer

Verle Muhrer is a philosophy instructor at Penn Valley Community College in Kansas City, Missouri. In the following viewpoint, he argues that beliefs in God, life after death, and reincarnation are all illusions that people use to lessen their fears of death. He asserts that such beliefs are detrimental to meaningful human living. Muhrer endorses a way of life that he calls eupraxophy, which emphasizes the present life rather than life after death.

As you read, consider the following questions:

1. Why does Muhrer contend that belief in an afterlife is harmful?
2. What should be the focus of funerals, according to the author?
3. How does Muhrer contrast religion and humanism?

Verle Muhrer, "A Eupraxophic Declaration on Death and Dying," *Free Inquiry*, Summer 1990. Reprinted with permission.

Death is a natural, not a supernatural phenomenon. It is a necessary component of all known forms of life on earth. It is to be understood and studied scientifically and naturally.

The hope and fear of rewards or punishments in the afterlife, in another life, or in a worldly reincarnation are contrary to the development of a realistic moral character and a healthy, ethical sense of justice.

The belief that the problem of death requires supernatural and religious solutions assumes that death itself is a supernatural phenomenon. It is not. No one is called from life to death by any supernatural forces. No god calls loved ones "home" because it is timely. Such claims made to the grieving are cruel and without a rational basis. Deaths are seldom timely and are nearly always too soon for the purpose of fulfillment of our life-goals.

A Vain Hope

All hope that death is not real and all hope for the afterlife is vain, immoral, perverse, and pathological.

No person claiming divine status has any special insights, by virtue of his or her claimed divine status, into the afterlife or reincarnation.

Neither life nor death is sacred or worthwhile for its own sake. The important question is, Which lives and which deaths are worthwhile and under what conditions? When Socrates said the unexamined life is not worth living, he clearly understood that there are humane preconditions necessary for the good life, two of which are rational inquiry and contemplation. Without these humane conditions present, we are indeed better off dead.

Death is not a punishment for human wrongdoing, nor is it the "wages of sin." Such a myth can only serve to produce irrational guilt and inhuman, servile dependence on irrational theologies of salvation, saviors, and messiahs, resurrected and divine.

Certainly not all deaths are good. Death does have a very real sting that is painful to the living, but this cannot be altered by theological illusions of immortality and divine salvation or by mad and irrational beliefs in reincarnation. In addition, such beliefs serve to reinforce socially exploitative relationships justified by the lie of karma, which says that the downtrodden desire and earn their status in the here and now by the deeds and thoughts of a previous life.

No person should be judged by the accident of an untimely death, any more than by the long-worn superstition of judging people by the accident of birth. Nor should the human race be judged as sinful because of the natural condition of dying.

The victory of the grave is no illusion. The grave is victorious.

In the end, it always has its way. To believe otherwise is vain, unrealistically prideful, self-deluding, and arrogant.

To be eupraxophic is to master not only living but death as well. We must have the courage and understanding to face our own mortality, and the mortalities of our loved ones and friends. However, secular humanists and eupraxophers are naturally more calm and less concerned about death because they understand it. Our fear, pain, and grief are tempered by aesthetic contemplation, reason, and human, not divine, acts of kindness, love, mercy, and comfort.

"This eternity—when is it all going to end?"

No illusion is authentically comforting, least of all the illusion that death is unreal and unnatural. (Not *really* real, not *really* natural and final, as nonsecularists and theists persistently tell us.) It is due to moral illusions, moral depravities, and moral deficiencies that we accept death as punishment or reward for sins and virtues for any one individual or group of individuals or for the human race. Death is *not* the wages of sin for our deficiencies now or for the original sins of our mythical first parents in a garden of paradise, long lost and past.

Traditional religion's placement of the unreality of death as central is not dignified. The perverse and obscene dread of death by traditional religion is obsessive, morbid, and destructive to human fulfillment in this life.

A death without religion is a viable, moral, and ethical alternative to death with religion. We believe it to be superior. The history of humanistic alternatives to death in the grasp of religion is rich and full. Eupraxophers from Socrates to the present have lived without religion and their deaths have been rounded and meaningful completions of their lives. We wish no intrusions of religion into our dying and into the dying of our loved ones. We believe such intrusions to be an affront to our rights and our dignity.

No Right to Kill

No worldly government or authority has the right to call on men and women to fight, kill, and die in military battle in a supernatural cause blessed by military chaplains or by anyone else claiming divine status or instrumentality. Religion has prospered in large measure because its professional representatives claiming a divine status have cynically manipulated those saddened by dying and death into signing over their wealth. We strenuously oppose this manipulation, and call for its cessation.

Ministers, mullahs, rabbis, priests, holy men and women, and the clergy have no special prerogatives over and above secularists, eupraxophers, and humanists to comfort the dying or to conduct ceremonies for the dead by virtue of their claims to divine status, calling, or anointing, or as instruments of the supernatural.

It is the responsibility of eupraxophers and secular humanists to conduct appropriate ceremonies for the dead and to comfort and give solace to the living. Eupraxophers should seize the presumed exclusive prerogative of the religious professionals to conduct ceremonies and rituals for the dead and to comfort the living.

It is a basic human right and a matter of elemental human dignity to have an inalienable power to control our own dying by suicide, euthanasia, or whatever means at our disposal. No state or religion can or should impose life on those who no longer find it worth living.

We encourage the scientific investigation and objective inquiry into the processes of dying and extinction, their relation to the overall history of life on earth, and their relationship to an overall understanding of evolution of life forms. We encourage scientific examination of claims of reincarnation, trance-channeling, spiritualism, near-death experiences, out-of-body experiences, discarnate spirits, ghosts, and all paranormal and religious claims capable of falsification or verification.

Given the present paucity of evidence for immortality, a carnate or discarnate afterlife, and a carnate rebirth in another body, we reject all claims of immortality as false and unproved based on hope and fear, not upon a healthy, rational life-stance.

We believe the care and compassionate support for the dying and the grief-stricken to be a paramount human responsibility. Appropriate secular and humanistic ceremonies should be conducted for the memory of what the dead stood for, lived for, loved for, and fought for. Such ceremonies are for the living and their purpose is not to invoke the supernatural and transcendent realm to provide better "accommodations" for the dead.

Religion's Cliches

We respect the right of joyful irreverence toward dying as a human response to the old and hoary supernatural dreads. Religion's vain and puerile attempt to deny death and provide a supernatural solution to a natural problem must be not only criticized, but made an object of humor seasoned with pungent sympathies for its many unwary victims. Religion's cliches of death seem to us simplistic, cold, horrific, and pompous. Against these pretenses we encourage jocularity. We accept and mourn the grim ironies and ghastly pains of dying and, yes, the sting and victory of death.

We will that religion's death dread die, and that eupraxophic exuberance endure and prevail.

Recognizing Statements That Are Provable

We are constantly confronted with statements and generalizations about social and moral problems. In order to think clearly about these problems, it is useful if one can make a basic distinction between statements for which evidence can be found and other statements which cannot be verified or proved because evidence is not available, or the issue is so controversial that it cannot be definitely proved.

Readers should be aware that magazines, newspapers, and other sources often contain statements of a controversial nature. The following activity is designed to allow experimentation with statements that are provable and those that are not.

The following statements are taken from the viewpoints in this chapter. Consider each statement carefully. *Mark P for any statement you believe is provable. Mark U for any statement you feel is unprovable because of the lack of evidence. Mark C for any statement you think is too controversial to be proved to everyone's satisfaction.*

If you are doing this activity as a member of a class or group, compare your answers with those of other class or group members. Be able to defend your answers. You may discover that others will come to different conclusions than you do. Listening to the reasons others present for their answers may give you valuable insights into recognizing statements that are provable.

P = provable
U = unprovable
C = too controversial

1. Human consciousness survives death.

2. There is no state of existence beyond this life.

3. The Roman philosopher Lucretius wrote about how both the mind and the body grow, develop, and age.

4. Karen Ann Quinlan lay in a coma for more than ten years before she finally died.

5. A 1984 *Newsweek* article on Alzheimer's Disease was entitled "A Slow Death of the Mind."

6. When the brain dies, the mind is gone forever.

7. Death is not a punishment for human wrongdoing.

8. All claims of immortality are false.

9. Several passages in the Bible point to the importance of the afterlife.

10. In many polls Americans have listed health as their number one priority, above love, work, and money.

11. The true meaning of life is found only by looking beyond this life.

12. According to a Gallup poll, more than eight million Americans have experienced near-death experiences.

13. Many NDE accounts have similar features, such as floating above one's body, rushing through a tunnel, and encountering beings of light.

14. Near-death experiences are descriptions of what happens after we die.

15. Many people who have had NDEs have found their lives transformed by the experience.

16. People who have experienced NDEs never really died, but just thought they did.

17. The stimulation of cells in the temporal lobe of the brain can produce instant experiences that seem like the reliving of memories.

18. Near-death experiences do not prove the existence of an afterlife.

Periodical Bibliography

The following articles have been selected to supplement the diverse views presented in this chapter.

A.J. Ayer	"What I Saw When I Was Dead," *National Review*, October 14, 1988.
Rodney Clapp	"Rumors of Heaven," *Christianity Today*, October 7, 1988.
Jonathan Cott	"Is There Life After Life?" *Vogue*, May 1987.
Timothy Ferris	"A Cosmological Event," *The New York Times Magazine*, December 15, 1991.
Verlyn Klinkenborg	"At the Edge of Eternity," *Life*, March 1992.
Paul Kurtz	"Scientific Evidence Keeps Us in the Here and Now," *Psychology Today*, September 1988.
Delos B. McKown	"Theological Mythologies and Naturalistic Certitudes," *Free Inquiry*, Summer 1990. Available from PO Box 664, Buffalo, NY 14226-0664.
Tim Madigan	"O Death, Where Is Thy Sting?" *Free Inquiry*, Summer 1990.
Charles Meyer	"Afterlife," *The Witness*, November 1990. Available from 1249 Washington Blvd., Suite 3115, Detroit, MI 48266-1868.
Melvin Morse	"Children of the Light," *Reader's Digest*, March 1991.
Pythia Peay	"Back from the Grave," *Utne Reader*, September/October 1991.
Paul Perry	"Brushes with Death," *Psychology Today*, September 1988.
Vernon Pizer	"To Beyond and Back," *The American Legion*, August 1991.
Charles Platt	"Explorations," *Omni*, February 1992.
Robert T. Reilly	"Heaven Can Wait: Do Near-Death Experiences Take the Fear Out of Dying?" *U.S. Catholic*, January 1988.
Nathan Schnaper and Harriet L. Panitz	"Near-Death Experiences: Perception *Is* Reality," *Journal of Near-Death Studies*, Winter 1990. Available from 233 Spring St., New York, NY 10013-1578.
Jacob Sullum	"Cold Comfort," *Reason*, April 1991.
William J. Whalen	"Reincarnation: Why Some People Expect to Make a Comeback," *U.S. Catholic*, August 1988.
Kenneth L. Woodward	"Heaven," *Newsweek*, March 27, 1989.

Organizations to Contact

The editors have compiled the following list of organizations that are concerned with the issues debated in this book. All have publications or information available for interested readers. For best results, allow as much time as possible for the organization to respond. The descriptions below are derived from materials provided by the organizations. This list was compiled upon the date of publication. Names, addresses, and phone numbers of organizations are subject to change.

American Life League (ALL)
PO Box 1350
Stafford, VA 22554
(703) 659-4171

ALL opposes abortion and euthanasia. It also opposes living wills and other advance directives on the grounds that they may lead to euthanasia. In addition to providing books, pamphlets, and other educational materials to the public, ALL publishes *Care of the Dying, Understanding Brain Death, The Living Will . . .?*, and the monthly newsletter *ALL About Issues.*

Association for Death Education and Counseling (ADEC)
638 Prospect Ave.
Hartford, CT 06105-4298
(203) 232-4825

ADEC is an interdisciplinary organization that addresses dying, death, and bereavement issues from the educator's and counselor's perspective. Its members include educators, physicians, counselors, hospice personnel, clergy, and social workers. The association works to assist professionals and lay people to better meet the needs of those they counsel, and seeks to promote research on death issues. It publishes the journal *Death Studies* and a newsletter *The Forum.*

Center for Death Education and Research
1167 Social Science Bldg.
University of Minnesota
267 19th Ave. S
Minneapolis, MN 55455
(612) 624-1895

The center sponsors research on grief and bereavement as well as studies of attitudes and responses to death and dying. It conducts classes and workshops for care-giving professionals. A list of published materials is available upon request.

The Center for the Rights of the Terminally Ill (CRTI)
PO Box 54246
Hurst, TX 76054
(817) 656-5143

CRTI is an educational, patient advocacy, and political action organization. Its main purposes are to help the sick and dying receive professional, competent, and ethical health care and to oppose euthanasia and assisted suicide through education and legislative action. It publishes the quarterly *CRTI Report*.

The Children's Legacy
PO Box 300305
Denver, CO 80203
(303) 830-7595

The Children's Legacy is an organization that works with terminally ill children. It helps these children create photojournals that help them document and deal with their feelings about death. The organization publishes brochures and *My Stupid Illness*, a workbook designed for use by children with serious illnesses.

Choice in Dying
250 W. 57th. St.
New York, NY 10107
(212) 246-6962

The organization distributes free living wills and other advance directives to those who request them and works to educate people about how to use such directives. It publishes a quarterly newsletter and publications on advance directives and end-of-life decision making. The organization was formed in 1991 from the merger of two groups: Concern for Dying and the Society for the Right to Die.

The Committee for the Scientific Investigation of Claims of the Paranormal (CSICOP)
PO Box 703
Buffalo, NY 14226-0703
(716) 636-1425

CSICOP attempts to encourage the critical investigation of paranormal phenomena from a scientific point of view. It has investigated and examined evidence for near-death experiences and reincarnation, and has generally found supporting evidence for such occurrences lacking or inconclusive. The organization publishes its findings in its quarterly journal *The Skeptical Inquirer.*

The Compassionate Friends (TCF)
PO Box 3696
Oak Brook, IL 60522-3696
(708) 990-0010

TCF is an informal self-help organization for parents who have experienced the death of a child. It sponsors support group meetings, publishes brochures, and distributes books on parental and sibling grief, including *We Need Not Walk Alone.*

Continental Association of Funeral and Memorial Societies, Inc. (CAFMS)
6900 Lost Lake Rd.
Egg Harbor, WI 54209
(800) 458-5563

CAFMS is a national association of local nonprofit organizations that focus on providing members with simple, dignified, and affordable cremations and burials. In addition to providing information on alternatives to expensive funerals, the association also publishes pamphlets on various death and dying issues, including the grieving process, living wills, and organ donation.

Dying with Dignity
600 Eglinton Ave. E, Suite 401
Toronto, Ontario, Canada M4P 1P3
(416) 486-3998

Dying with Dignity distributes living wills and other advance directive forms to Canadians. It seeks to educate the public and health-care professionals about protecting a patient's personal autonomy when making treatment decisions for the dying. It publishes a brochure *Dying with Dignity* and a quarterly newsletter.

Elisabeth Kübler-Ross Center
South Route 616
Head Waters, VA 24442
(703) 396-3441

The center, directed by well-known author and counselor Elisabeth Kübler-Ross, conducts a variety of workshops and retreats on death, terminal illness, AIDS, and bereavement. It publishes a periodic newsletter and brochures on death and dying.

The Foundation of Thanatology
630 W. 168th St.
New York, NY 10032
(212) 928-2066

This organization of health, theology, psychology, and social science professionals is devoted to scientific and humanist inquiries into death, loss, grief, and bereavement. The foundation, formed in 1967, coordinates professional, educational, and research programs concerned with mortality and grief. It publishes annual directories and the periodicals *Advances in Thanatology* and *Archives of the Foundation of Thanatology.*

The Hastings Center
255 Elm Rd.
Briarcliff Manor, NY 10510
(914) 762-8500

Since its founding in 1969, the Hastings Center has examined the ethical and legal ramifications of advances in medicine, the biological sciences, and the social and behavioral sciences. The center's three goals are to promote research on these issues, stimulate universities and schools to support the teaching of ethics, and educate the public concerning these issues. Among the issues it has examined are the definition of death and the use of advance directives in the care of terminal patients. It publishes the bimonthly *Hastings Center Report.*

The Hemlock Society
PO Box 11830
Eugene, OR 97440-3900
(503) 342-5748

The society supports active voluntary euthanasia for the terminally ill and believes that the final decision to end one's life is one's own. It does not encourage suicide for anyone who is not terminally ill, and it supports suicide prevention programs. It sells books on death and dying, including *Final Exit*, a guide to those who are suffering from terminal illnesses and are considering suicide. The society also distributes living wills and publishes the *Hemlock Quarterly*, a newsletter with information on death and dying.

Hospice Education Institute (HEI)
PO Box 713
Essex, CT 06426-0713
(800) 331-1620

HEI provides information to health-care professionals and the public on hospice care and bereavement counseling. It maintains a computerized directory of hospices in the United States and provides referrals to local hospice programs. The institute also publishes books and pamphlets on hospice-related subjects.

International Association for Near-Death Studies (IANDS)
638 Prospect Ave.
Hartford, CT 06105-4298
(203) 232-4825

IANDS is a worldwide organization of scientists, scholars, and others who are interested in or have had near-death experiences. It supports the scientific study of near-death experiences and their implications, fosters communication among researchers on this topic, and sponsors support groups in which people can discuss their near-death experiences. The association publishes the quarterly *Journal of Near-Death Studies*.

Make Today Count (MTC)
168 Panoramic
Camdenton, MO 65065
(314) 346-6644

MTC is an international organization that provides emotional support to people with life-threatening illnesses and to their family and friends. It published the book *Make Today Count—Until Tomorrow Comes* and distributes a bimonthly newsletter.

National Funeral Directors Association (NFDA)
11121 W. Oklahoma Ave.
Milwaukee, WI 53227
(414) 541-2500

NFDA is a federation of state funeral directors' associations. It provides seminars and publishes the monthly magazine *The Director*. It also distributes numerous pamphlets on death and dying, funeral planning, hospice care, and the grieving process.

National Hospice Organization (NHO)
1901 N. Moore St., Suite 901
Arlington, VA 22209
(703) 243-5900

The organization serves as an advocacy group for and information clearinghouse on hospices in the United States It publishes the annual *Guide to the Nation's Hospices* and the quarterly *Hospice Journal*.

THEOS Foundation
717 Liberty Ave.
Pittsburgh, PA 15222
(412) 471-7779

The THEOS (They Help Each Other Spiritually) Foundation provides education and support groups for widowed people. It provides a bibliography of books and other resources on bereavement and publishes the *Survivors Outreach Magazine* series and the brochure *Grief Is Not a Sign of Weakness*.

Bibliography of Books

Mark Albrecht — *Reincarnation: A Christian Approach to a New Age Doctrine.* Downers Grove, IL: Inter-Varsity Press, 1987.

Patricia Anderson — *Affairs in Order: A Complete Resource Guide to Death and Dying.* New York: Macmillan, 1991.

George J. Annas — *The Rights of Patients: The Basic ACLU Guide to Patients' Rights.* 2nd ed. Carbondale, IL: American Civil Liberties Union Handbooks, Southern University Press, 1989.

Arnold R. Beisser — *A Graceful Passage: Notes on the Freedom to Live or Die.* New York: Doubleday, 1990.

Arthur Berger et al., eds. — *Perspectives on Death and Dying.* Philadelphia: The Charles Press, 1989.

Eric Blau — *Common Heroes: Facing a Life Threatening Illness.* Pasadena, CA: NewSage Press, 1989.

Robert Buckman — *I Don't Know What to Say: How to Help and Support Someone Who Is Dying.* Toronto: Key Porter Books, 1988.

Daniel Callahan — *What Kind of Life: The Limits of Medical Progress.* New York: Simon and Schuster, 1990.

Lisa Carlson — *Caring for Your Own Dead.* Hinesburg, VT: Upper Access Publishers, 1987.

B.D. Colen — *The Essential Guide to a Living Will.* New York: Simon and Schuster, 1991.

Melba Colgrove, Harold H. Bloomfield, and Peter McWilliams — *How to Survive the Loss of a Love.* Rev. ed. Los Angeles: Prelude Press, 1991.

Stanley P. Cornils — *The Mourning After: How to Manage Grief Wisely.* Saratoga, CA: R&E Publishers, 1990.

David A. Crenshaw — *Bereavement: Counseling the Grieving Throughout the Life Cycle.* New York: Continuum, 1990.

Stephen T. Davis — *Death and Afterlife.* London: Macmillan, 1989.

Rosemary Dinnage — *The Ruffian on the Stair: Reflections on Death.* New York: Viking, 1990.

Gary Doore, ed. — *What Survives? Contemporary Explorations of Life After Death.* Los Angeles: Jeremy P. Tarcher, 1990.

Deborah Duda — *Coming Home: A Guide to Dying at Home with Dignity.* New York: Aurora Press, 1987.

Sara Engram — *Mortal Matters: When a Loved One Dies.* Kansas City, MO: Andrews and McMeel, 1990.

David Feinstein and Peg Elliott Mayo — *Rituals for Living and Dying.* New York: HarperCollins Publishers, 1990.

Martin Gardner — *The New Age: Notes of a Fringe Watcher.* Buffalo, NY: Prometheus Books, 1988.

Karen G. Gervais — *Redefining Death.* New Haven, CT: Yale University Press, 1986.

Samuel Gorovitz — *Drawing the Line: Life, Death and Ethical Choices in an American Hospital.* New York: Oxford University Press, 1991.

| Billy Graham | *Facing Death and the Life After*. Irving, TX: Word Books, 1987. |

Earl A. Grollman — *Talking About Death: A Dialogue Between Parent and Child*. 3rd ed. Boston: Beacon Press, 1990.

Chris Hackler, Ray Moseley, and Dorothy E. Vawter, eds. — *Advance Directives in Medicine*. New York: Praeger Press, 1989.

Barbara Harris and Lionel C. Bascom — *Full Circle: The Near-Death Experience and Beyond*. New York: Pocket Books, 1990.

Christopher Jay Johnson and Marsha G. McGee, eds. — *How Different Religions View Death and Afterlife*. Philadelphia: The Charles Press, 1991.

Philip Kapleau — *The Wheel of Life and Death*. New York: Doubleday, 1989.

Michael C. Kearl — *Endings: A Sociology of Death and Dying*. New York: Oxford University Press, 1989.

Barry S. Kogan, ed. — *A Time to Be Born and a Time to Die: The Ethics of Choice*. Hawthorne, NY: Aldine de Gruyter, 1991.

Kenneth Kramer — *The Sacred Art of Dying*. New York: Paulist Press, 1988.

Elisabeth Kübler-Ross — *Working It Through*. New York: Macmillan, 1987.

David Lamb — *Death, Brain Death, and Ethics*. London: Croom Helm, 1988.

Michael R. Leming and George E. Dickinson — *Understanding Dying, Death, and Bereavement*. 2nd ed. Orlando, FL: Holt, Rinehart and Winston, 1990.

Michael Lesy — *The Forbidden Zone*. New York: Doubleday, 1989.

Stephen Levine — *Healing into Life and Death*. New York: Doubleday, 1989.

Audre Lorde — *A Burst of Light*. Ithaca, NY: Firebrand Books, 1988.

Alan Meisal — *The Right to Die*. New York: John Wiley and Sons, 1989.

Raymond A. Moody Jr. — *The Light Beyond.* New York: Bantam Books, 1988.

Vincent Mor, David S. Greer, and Robert Kastenbaum, eds. — *The Hospice Experiment*. Baltimore: The Johns Hopkins University Press, 1988.

John D. Morgan, ed. — *Young People and Death*. Philadelphia: The Charles Press, 1991.

Melvin Morse and Paul Perry — *Closer to the Light*. New York: Villard Books, 1990.

Elizabeth Harper Neeld — *Seven Choices*. New York: Clarkson N. Potter, 1990.

Danai Papadatou and Costas Papadatos, eds. — *Children and Death*. New York: Hemisphere Publishing, 1991.

Peter Prunkl and Rebecca L. Berry — *Death Week: Exploring the Dying Process*. New York: Hemisphere Publishing, 1989.

Gilda Radner — *It's Always Something*. New York: Simon and Schuster, 1989.

Robert L. Risley — *Death With Dignity*. Eugene, OR: The Hemlock Society, 1989.

D. Scott Rogo — *Life After Death: The Case for Survival of Bodily Death.*

	Wellingborough, Great Britain: The Aquarian Press, 1987.
Elliott J. Rosen	*Families Facing Death*. Lexington, MA: Lexington Books, 1990.
Dorothy T. Samuel	*Grieving: An Inward Journey*. St. Cloud, MN: North Star Press, 1988.
Cicely Saunders and Mary Baines	*Living with Dying: The Management of Terminal Disease*. 2nd ed. New York: Oxford University Press, 1989.
Thomas and Celia Scully	*Making Medical Decisions: How to Make Difficult Medical and Ethical Choices for Yourself and Your Family*. New York: Simon and Schuster, 1989.
Bradley E. Smith	*Write Your Own Living Will*. New York: Crown Publishing, 1991.
Harry Van Bommel	*Choices: For People Who Have a Terminal Illness, Their Families and Caregivers*. Toronto: NC Press Limited, 1990.
Robert M. Veatch	*Death, Dying and the Biological Revolution: Our Last Quest for Responsibility*. Rev. Ed. New Haven, CT: Yale University Press, 1989.
Dietrich von Hildebrand	*Jaws of Death: Gate of Heaven*. Manchester, NH: Sophia Institute Press, 1991.
Froma Walsh and Monica McGoldrick, eds.	*Living Beyond Loss: Death in the Family*. New York: W.W. Norton & Company, 1991.
Hannelore Wass, Felix M. Berardo, and Robert A. Neimeyer, eds.	*Dying: Facing the Facts*. 2nd Ed. New York: Hemisphere Publishing, 1988.
Colin Wilson	*Afterlife*. Garden City, NY: Doubleday & Co., 1987.
Carol G. Zaleski	*Otherworld Journeys: Accounts of Near-Death Experiences in Medieval and Modern Times*. New York: Oxford University Press, 1987.
Richard M. Zaner, ed.	*Death: Beyond Whole-Brain Criteria*. Boston: Kluwer Academic Publishers, 1988.

Index

234